The Oak-tree Fairy Book; Favorite Fairy Tales

THE OAK–TREE FAIRY BOOK

FAVORITE FAIRY TALES

EDITED BY

CLIFTON JOHNSON

ILLUSTRATED BY

WILLARD BONTE

BOSTON

LITTLE, BROWN, AND COMPANY

1905

Published November, 1905

Printers
S. J. PARKHILL & CO., BOSTON, U. S. A.

INTRODUCTORY NOTE

HERE are the old favorites in a version especially suited for the home fireside. The interest, the charm, and all the sweetness have been retained; but savagery, distressing details, and excessive pathos have been dropped. Surely our little people are better off without some of the sentiments of that barbaric past when the tales originated. Felix Adler, in his notable work on "The Moral Education of Children," years ago appealed for just such a version as this, wherein there should be "less of falsehood, gluttony, drunkenness, and evil in general" than in the usual tellings, and from which "malicious stepmothers and cruel fathers should be excluded." The same need has been widely felt by parents and teachers. "The Oak-Tree Fairy Book" supplies this want, and can be read aloud or placed in the hands of the children with entire confidence. The changes are not, however, very radical in most instances, and I have made no alteration in incidents where there did not seem to be an ethical necessity for so doing.

The first sixteen tales in this book have a special claim to the attention of American readers, for they were picked up in this country. Two or three of them are to be found in nearly all our fairy-tale collections, and it would not be safe to say that any of them originated here; yet there are none of the sixteen but that differ in an interesting way from the usual versions, and most of them are quite unfamiliar to the present generation. I am indebted for them to friends and correspondents and to the *American Journal of Folk Lore*. Readers acquainted with similar tales not in the ordinary collections will confer a favor if they will communicate with me.

CLIFTON JOHNSON

Hadley, Mass.

If the stories you read in the following pages and the pictures that illustrate them please you, watch for " The Birch-Tree Fairy Book " next year.

CONTENTS

LIST OF ILLUSTRATIONS

THE OAK-TREE FAIRY BOOK

JOHNNY-CAKE

ONCE upon a time there was an old man and an old woman and a little boy. One morning the old man got up and started the kitchen fire, and the old woman got up and made a Johnny-cake and put it in the oven to bake it.

The little boy slept in the kitchen, and the old woman shook him to awaken him, and said, "Your father and I are going out to work in the garden, and do you get up, and pretty soon you must turn the Johnny-cake."

So the old man and old woman went out, and began to hoe potatoes in the garden and left the little boy to watch the oven; but the little boy was lazy, and he lay snug and warm in bed, half asleep.

By-and-by he said to himself, "Oh, dear, I shall have to get up to turn the Johnny-cake!"

But the Johnny-cake called out, "No, you need n't; I can turn myself."

The little boy was not sure about that, and he

scrambled out of bed and began to dress; but he had only got his trousers on when he saw the oven-door swing back, and out jumped Johnny-cake and started toward the open door of the house. The little boy ran to shut the door, but Johnny-cake was too quick for him and was down the steps and out into the road before the little boy could catch him.

"Johnny-cake's running away, Johnny-cake's running away!" shouted the little boy, and hurried after him as fast as he could scamper, and the old man and old woman threw down their hoes and hastened to join in the chase.

But Johnny-cake outran all three, and shortly was gone from sight, and his pursuers sat down, panting for breath, on a bank to rest.

On went Johnny-cake, and by-and-by he came to four mowers in a meadow, who looked up from their work and called out, "Where are ye going, Johnny-cake?"

"Oh," said Johnny-cake, "I've outrun an old man and an old woman and a little boy, and I can outrun you, *too-o-o!*"

"Ye can, can ye? We'll see about that!" said they, and they threw down their scythes and ran after him; but they could not catch up with him, and presently they had to sit down by the road-side to rest.

On ran Johnny-cake, and by-and-by he came to two ditch-diggers, who were digging a ditch.

"Where are ye going, Johnny-cake?" they asked.

"Oh," said he, "I've outrun an old man and an old woman and a little boy and four mowers, and I can outrun you, *too-o-o!*"

"Ye can, can ye? We'll see about that!" said they, and they threw down their spades and ran after him; but Johnny-cake soon outstripped them, and, seeing they could never catch him, they gave up the chase and sat down to rest.

On went Johnny-cake, and by-and-by he came to a bear.

"Where are ye going, Johnny-cake?" the bear asked.

"Oh," said Johnny-cake, "I've outrun an old man and an old woman and a little boy and four mowers and two ditch-diggers, and I can outrun you, *too-o-o!*"

"Ye can, can ye? We'll see about that!" growled the bear, and hurried as fast as his legs could carry him after Johnny-cake, who kept right on along the road.

Pretty soon the bear was left so far behind that he saw he might as well give up the hunt first as last. So he stretched himself by the wayside to rest.

On went Johnny-cake, and by-and-by he came to a wolf.

"Where are ye going, Johnny-cake?" the wolf asked.

"Oh," said Johnny-cake, "I've outrun an old man and an old woman and a little boy and four mowers and two ditch-diggers and a bear, and I can outrun you, *too-o-o!*"

"Ye can, can ye? We'll see about that!" snarled the wolf; and he set off at a gallop after Johnny-cake, who went on and on so fast that the wolf soon saw there was no hope of catching him, and lay down to rest.

On went Johnny-cake, and by-and-by he came to a fox, who was stretched out for a nap among some bushes a little aside from the road.

The fox heard Johnny-cake coming, and he cried out in a sharp voice, without getting up, "Where are ye going, Johnny-cake?"

"Oh," said Johnny-cake, "I've outrun an old

man and an old woman and a little boy and four
mowers and two ditch-diggers and a bear and a wolf,
and I can outrun you, *too-o-o!* "

The fox said, " I can't quite hear ye, Johnny-
cake. Won't ye come a little closer? "

So Johnny-cake went a little closer, and called
out in a very loud voice, " *I 've outrun an old man
and an old woman and a little boy and four mowers and
two ditch-diggers and a bear and a wolf, and I can outrun you,* TOO-O-O ! ' "

" I can't quite hear ye. Won't ye come a little
closer? " said the fox, putting a paw behind one of
his ears to help him hear better.

So Johnny-cake came up quite close, and screamed
out still louder, " I 'VE OUTRUN AN OLD MAN AND
AN OLD WOMAN AND A LITTLE BOY AND FOUR
MOWERS AND TWO DITCH-DIGGERS AND A BEAR AND
A WOLF, AND I CAN OUTRUN YOU, TOO-O-O ! "

"Ye can, can ye?" yelped the fox, and he snapped up Mr. Johnny-cake in his sharp teeth and ate him; and that was the end of poor Johnny-cake.

The bear hurried as fast as his legs could carry him after Johnny-cake.

THE TWIST-MOUTH FAMILY

THERE was once a father and a mother and several children, and all but one of them had their mouths twisted out of shape. The one whose mouth was not twisted was a son named John.

When John got to be a young man he was sent to college, and on the day he came home for his first vacation the family sat up late in the evening to hear him tell of all he had learned. But finally they prepared to go to bed, and the mother said, " Father, will you blow out the light ? "

" Yes, I will," was his reply.

" Well, I wish you would," said she.

" Well, I will," he said.

So he blew, but his mouth was twisted and he blew upward, this way — and he could n't blow out the light.

Then he said, " Mother, will you blow out the light ? "

" Yes, I will," was her reply.

" Well, I wish you would," said he.

" Well, I will," she said.

So she blew, but her mouth was twisted and she blew downward, this way — and she could n't blow out the light.

Then she spoke to her daughter and said, " Mary, will you blow out the light? "

" Yes, I will," was Mary's reply.

" Well, I wish you would," said her mother.

" Well, I will," Mary said.

So Mary blew, but her mouth was twisted and she blew out of the right corner of her mouth, this way — and she could n't blow out the light.

Then Mary spoke to one of her brothers and said, " Dick, will you blow out the light? "

" Yes, I will," was Dick's reply.

" Well, I wish you would," said Mary.

" Well, I will," Dick said.

So Dick blew, but his mouth was twisted, and he blew out of the left corner of his mouth, this way — and he could n't blow out the light.

Then Dick said, "John, will you blow out the light?"

"Yes, I will," was John's reply.

"Well, I wish you would," said Dick.

"Well, I will," John said.

So John blew, and his mouth was not twisted and he blew straight, this way — and he blew out the light.

The light was out, and they were all glad that John had succeeded, and the father said, "What a blessed thing it is to have larnin'!"

THE TALE OF A BLACK CAT

ONCE there was a little boy named Tommy; and there's a ⊤ . That stands for Tommy.

Tommy's house was not a very good one. So he built a new wall on this side of it.

And then he built a new wall on that side of it.

You can see now that he had two nice rooms in his house, though not very large. Next he put in windows to look out of — one in this room — and one in that room.

Then he made a tall chimney on this side of his house.

And then he made a tall chimney on the other side of his house.

After that he started some grass beside his door, like this. Not far away from Tommy's house lived a little girl named Sally; and there's an ſ . That stands for Sally.

When Tommy had finished his house he thought
he would like to go and tell Sally what he had been

doing, so he came out
of his door and walked
along, this way, over to
where she lived.

Sally was glad to see him, and he went into
the kitchen and sat down and explained to her
how he had built two new walls to his house
and put in windows and made two tall chim-
neys, and how he had started the grass in front
of his door. "And now, Sally," said he, "I want
you to come over and see how well I've fixed
things."

"I'll put on my bonnet and go right back with
you," said Sally; but when she was ready to start
she said, "We might go down cellar first and get
some apples to eat on the way."

So they went down cellar, like this.

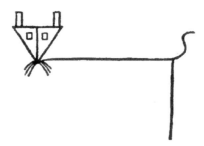

They got some apples, and then they came up outdoors by the hatchway, like this.

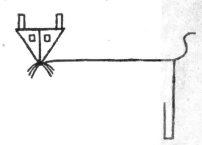

Now they started for Tommy's house, but the walking was bad, and they had gone only a few steps when they tumbled down, like this.

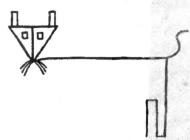

However, they were quickly up, like this.

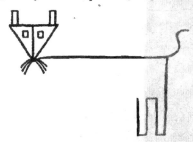

And they walked along until they were nearly to

Tommy's house when they tumbled down again, like this.

And they were no sooner up on their feet, like this,

than they tumbled down once more, like this.

But they were nearly to Tommy's house now, and

they got up and were going into the yard straight toward the door, like this,

— when Sally pointed toward the doorstep and cried out, " O-o-o-o-o-o-oh! See that big BLACK CAT!"

THE TALKING EGGS

THERE was once a girl named Blanche, and when she was ten years old her father and mother died, and she went to live with an aunt who had a daughter Rose. This daughter was selfish and disagreeable, and yet her mother did everything she could for her; while she treated Blanche, who was pleasant and obliging, very badly. Rose could sit all day long in a rocking-chair and do nothing if she chose, but Blanche was kept constantly at work, and had to eat in the kitchen. Among other things, she was obliged to go twice a day to bring water from a well more than a mile and a half distant from the house.

One morning, when she approached the well with her bucket, she found an old woman standing beside the well who said, "Pray, my little one, give me a drink, for I am very thirsty."

2

"That I will do gladly," replied Blanche, and she drew from the well a nice fresh bucketful.

The old woman drank, and then said, "Thank you, my child, you are a good girl, and I shall not forget your kindness."

A few days afterward Blanche was used so roughly by her aunt that she ran away into the woods. She was afraid to return home, and she sat down at the foot of a great tree and cried, and knew not what to do. But pretty soon she saw the old woman who had spoken to her at the well coming toward her.

"Ah, my child," said the old woman, "why are you crying? What has hurt you?"

"My aunt, with whom I live, has beaten me," Blanche answered, "and I am afraid to go home."

"Well, my dear," the old woman said, "come with me, and I will give you some supper and a bed; but you must promise not to laugh at anything you will see."

Blanche promised, and the old woman took her by the hand and they walked on deeper into the woods until they arrived at the old woman's cabin. When they went inside the old woman said, "Now you make a fire, my child, to cook the supper for us."

While Blanche made the fire the old woman sat
down in her chair beside the hearth and took off her
head, and after adjusting it carefully on her knees
she combed her hair. Blanche thought that very
strange, and she was a little frightened, but she said
nothing.

Presently the old woman set her head back on
her shoulders and went to a cupboard and took out
a large bone. "Here," said she, handing the bone
to Blanche, "put this in the pot
that hangs on the crane."

Blanche put the bone in the pot,
and lo! in a moment the pot was
full of good meat. Then
the old woman gave
Blanche a grain of rice
and said, "You see that
wooden mortar in the cor-
ner with the pestle
in it? Put this grain
of rice into the mor-
tar and pound it."

So Blanche put the
grain of rice into the
mortar and began to
pound it, and imme-

diately the mortar was full of rice, and this they cooked, and had it and the meat for their supper.

The next morning, after breakfast, the old woman said to Blanche, "You must now return home, but, as you are a good girl, I want to make you a pres- . ent of some talking eggs. Go to the chicken-house, and all the eggs which say 'Take me!' you may carry away with you; and all those which say 'Do not take me!' you must leave. When you are on your way home throw the eggs behind your back to break them."

Blanche did just as she was bidden. She went to the chicken-house, and the eggs in the nests began to speak, and some said, "Take me!" and some said, "Do not take me!" Those that said "Take me!" she put in her apron and carried away with her, and when she had walked to the borders of the forest she stopped and threw the eggs one by one behind her back.

Many pretty things came out of those eggs — diamonds, gold, beautiful dresses, and, lastly, a splendid carriage with two fine horses and a driver. She put the dresses and diamonds and gold into the carriage, and then got in herself and was driven home; and you may be sure her aunt was very much surprised to see her when she came with such riches, and wanted to know where she got them.

So Blanche told how she had met the old woman in the woods, and how the old woman took her home and kept her over night, and how in the morning the old woman had given her the talking eggs that were no sooner broken than there came forth from them all the wonderful things she had brought home.

Her aunt was far from pleased that Blanche should have so much and her own daughter so little, and the next day she said, " Rose, you must go to the forest, now, and look for that same old woman, for I want you to have as many nice things as Blanche has."

The plan suited Rose very well, and she went to the woods and wandered about until she met the old woman. It was then late in the afternoon, and Rose said, " Please, ma'am, will you take me home with you? It is a long way to my own home."

" Yes," said the old woman, " you can go with me, for it is almost dark, but you must not laugh at anything you see."

So they walked on deeper into the woods until they arrived at the old woman's cabin. They went inside, and when the old woman sat down and took off her head to comb her hair Rose laughed. Rose laughed, too, at all the other things she saw that were strange, and tried to make funny remarks about them.

" Ah! my child," said the old woman, " you are not a good girl, and I fear you will be punished for your actions."

The next morning the old woman gave Rose her breakfast, and then told her she must return home. Rose started at once, but as soon as she was outside the cabin she went to the old woman's chicken-house, saying to herself, " I must have some of those talking eggs before I go."

She opened the door, and the eggs in the nests immediately began to speak, and some said, " Take me!" and some said, " Do not take me!"

" Oh, yes!" exclaimed Rose, " I understand your tricks, and I shan't bother myself with you that say ' Take me!' It's the others I want, and you may say ' Don't take me!' all you please, but you are the very ones I shall carry away with me."

So she took all the eggs that told her not to take them, and went off with them in her apron. At the edge of the forest she threw them behind her back, and out of them came a lot of snakes, toads, and frogs. Rose ran and shrieked, and the snakes

The snakes and toads and frogs followed her all the way home

and toads and frogs followed after her all the way
home. She reached her mother's so tired she could
hardly speak, and had just strength left to shut the
door behind her and keep out all the dreadful
creatures that had chased her.

"Oh, mercy!" exclaimed her mother, when Rose
told her what had happened; "it is that wretch
Blanche who is the cause of all this, and she shall
be punished as she deserves."

So she called Blanche, and said to her, "Take
your things and get out of the house. You shall
not live with us any longer."

There was nothing for Blanche to do but to
call for her coach, and put into it the fine
dresses and diamonds and gold she had got
from the talking eggs, and then drive away.
She took a road that passed through the forest,
and it happened that the king's son was hunting there, and she met him on his horse.
When he saw the beautiful girl weeping in
the carriage, he asked her why she cried.

"Alas!" said she, "I have been
turned out of the house that has
been my home,
and I know not
where to go."

The prince tried to console her, and as they talked he became so charmed with her beauty and innocence that he asked her to be his wife. Then they went home together to the king's palace, and there they lived happily ever after.

THE TRAVELS OF A FOX

ONE day a fox was digging behind a stump and he found a bumblebee; and the fox put the bumblebee in a bag and took the bag over his shoulder and travelled.

At the first house he came to he went in and said to the mistress of the house, "Can I leave my bag here while I go to Squintum's?"

"Yes," said the woman.

"Then be careful not to open the bag," said the fox.

But as soon as he was out of sight the woman said to herself, "Well, I wonder what the fellow has in his bag that he is so careful about. I will look and see. It can't do any harm, for I shall tie the bag right up again."

However, the moment she unloosed the string out flew the bumblebee, and the rooster caught him and ate him all up.

After a while the fox came back. He took up his bag and knew at once that his bumblebee was gone, and he said to the woman, "Where is my bumblebee?"

And the woman said, "I untied the string just to take a little peep to find out what was in your bag, and the bumblebee flew out and the rooster ate him."

"Very well," said the fox; "I must have the rooster, then."

So he caught the rooster and put him in his bag and travelled.

At the next house he came to he went in and said to the mistress of the house, "Can I leave my bag here while I go to Squintum's?"

"Yes," said the woman.

"Then be careful not to open the bag," said the fox.

But as soon as he was out of sight the woman said to herself, "Well, I wonder what the fellow has in his bag that he is so careful about. I will look and see. It can't do any harm, for I shall tie the bag right up again."

However, the moment she unloosed the string the rooster flew out and the pig caught him and ate him all up.

After a while the fox came back. He took up his bag and knew at once that his rooster was gone, and he said to the woman, "Where is my rooster?"

And the woman said, "I untied the string just to take a little peep to find out what was in your bag, and the rooster flew out and the pig ate him."

"Very well," said the fox, "I must have the pig, then."

So he caught the pig and put him in his bag and travelled.

At the next house he came to he went in and said to the mistress of the house, "Can I leave my bag here while I go to Squintum's?"

"Yes," said the woman.

"Then be careful not to open the bag," said the-fox.

But as soon as he was out of sight the woman said to herself, "Well, I wonder what the fellow has in his bag that he is so careful about. I will look and see. It can't do any harm, for I shall tie the bag right up again."

However, the moment she unloosed the string the pig jumped out and the ox gored him.

After a while the fox came back. He took up his bag and knew at once that his pig was gone, and he said to the woman, "Where is my pig?"

And the woman said, "I untied the string just to take a little peep to find out what was in your bag, and the pig jumped out and the ox gored him."

"Very well," said the fox, "I must have the ox, then."

So he caught the ox and put him in his bag and travelled.

At the next house he came to he went in and said to the mistress of the house, "Can I leave my bag here while I go to Squintum's?"

"Yes," said the woman.

"Then be careful not to open the bag," said the fox.

But as soon as he was out of sight the woman said to herself, "Well, I wonder what the fellow has in his bag that he is so careful about. I will look and see. It can't do any harm, for I shall tie the bag right up again."

However, the moment she unloosed the string the ox got out, and the woman's little boy chased the ox out of the house and across a meadow and over a hill, clear out of sight.

After a while the fox came back. He took up his bag and knew at once that his ox was gone, and he said to the woman, " Where is my ox ? "

And the woman said, " I untied the string just to take a little peep to find out what was in your bag, and the ox got out and my little boy chased him out of the house and across a meadow and over a hill, clear out of sight."

"Very well," said the fox, " I must have the little boy, then."

So he caught the little boy and put him in his bag and travelled.

At the next house he came to he went in and said to the mistress of the house, " Can I leave my bag here while I go to Squintum's ? "

" Yes," said the woman.

" Then be careful not to open the bag," said the fox.

The woman had been making cake, and when it was baked she took it from the oven, and her children gathered around her teasing for some of it.

"Oh, ma, give me a piece!" said one, and "Oh, ma, give me a piece!" said each of the others.

And the smell of the cake came to the little boy in the bag, and he heard the children beg for the cake, and he said, "Oh, mammy, give me a piece!"

Then the woman opened the bag and took the little boy out; and she put the house-dog in the bag in the little boy's place, and the little boy joined the other children.

After a while the fox came back. He took up his bag and he saw that it was tied fast and he thought that the little boy was safe inside. "I have been all day on the road," said he, "without a thing to eat, and I am getting hungry. I will just step off into the woods now and see how this little boy I have in my bag tastes."

So he put the bag on his back and travelled deep into the woods. Then he sat down and untied the bag, and if the little boy had been in there things would have gone badly with him.

But the little boy was at the house of the woman who made the cake, and when the fox untied the bag the house-dog jumped out and killed him.

JACK AND THE BEAN-STALK

LONG, long ago there lived a poor widow who had a little boy named Jack. It was not easy for the woman to get a living; but she owned a cow that gave a great deal of milk, and some of the milk they drank and some she sold. So they contrived to get along until at last the cow went dry.

"What shall I do now?" said the woman sorrowfully, and she was ready to weep.

"Cheer up, mother," said Jack; "I will go and get work."

"You are too small," replied his mother. "No one would hire you. Ah, well, I must take our cow to market and sell her."

So the woman tied a rope to the cow's horns and led her away; but she had not gone far when she met a funny-looking old man who stopped and said, "Good-morning, madam."

"Good-morning to you," was her response.

"And where are you off to this morning?" asked the old man.

"I am going to market to sell my cow," the woman answered.

"If that is the case," said the old man, "I'll save you the trouble of going any farther, for I will buy your cow right here."

"And how much will you give me for her?" inquired the woman.

Then the old man took a little bag from his pocket and opened it for her to look inside; but all she saw in the bag was a handful of beans. "I will give you these beans for your cow," said the old man.

"I would rather not make such an exchange as that," the woman said. "Those beans would not be enough for one meal."

"Oh, they are not for you to eat!" exclaimed the old man. "You must plant them. They are magic beans that will bring you good luck, and they are worth much more than your cow."

The woman looked again, and she saw that the beans were very curious and of many pretty colors; and at last she said she would take them and let the old man have the cow. But on her way home, the more she thought about what she had done the more foolish she thought she had been, and when she reached the house she poured the beans out into her hand to look at them, and then threw them into the fireplace.

"I can't bear the sight of them," said she, "and now we shall soon starve, I suppose."

She thought that was the last of the beans, but one of them had rolled out across the floor, and the next day as she was sweeping she swept up the little bean. She did not notice it, and she swept it along and along and might have swept it into the fireplace; but her little boy Jack saw it and he picked it up and said, "I'm going to plant this bean, mother."

So he took it out to the garden and dug a hole and planted it. After that he was all the time running out to see if his bean had come up, and when it did come up he was all the time running out to see how it was growing.

On the first morning after he planted it he found its first leaves had already pushed their way up out of the ground. The next morning it was as tall as he was; and the next day after that it was as high as the house, and the next day after that it was as high as the church steeple. So it kept growing until its top was clear out of sight.

Then Jack said, "I'm going to climb this bean-stalk," and he climbed and climbed and climbed, and at last he reached the sky.

There he found a strange country without a tree, shrub, house, or living creature anywhere in sight. He sat down on a stone to rest and said, "Humph! if this is all there is up here I may as well go back home."

But while he was resting he noticed that a rough path led away from near where he sat over a hill, and then he saw a beautiful lady walking along the path toward him. She spoke to Jack as soon as she came to him, and he rose and took off his hat. "I am a fairy," said she, "and the country where you now are is on the borders of Fairy-land. I have come to tell you something about your father. Do you remember him?"

"No," replied Jack, "and when I ask my mother about him she always begins to cry and will say nothing."

"I thought as much," said the fairy, "and you will understand why your mother never speaks of him when you hear my story. He was a brave and generous knight, and the fairies were his friends and made him many wonderful presents. But after a time a wicked giant came to your father's castle and killed him, and carried off all the wonderful things the fairies had given him. At the same time the giant carried off your mother and you, who were then a little baby. He shut you both up in one of his dungeons, but at last he offered to restore your mother and you to liberty on condition that she should never speak about her wrongs to any one. She agreed, and he carried her to a place a great distance from where she had lived and been known before, and left her there with just money enough to rent a little cottage and buy a cow.

"That giant lives in this country, and if you follow the path by which you saw me come you will find his castle over yonder hill. All that he has is rightfully yours, and perhaps you can contrive some way to regain possession of what he stole from your father."

Then the fairy went on her way, and Jack, after thinking things over, concluded he would go on by the path that led toward the hill. Beyond the hill in a valley he came to a great castle, and on the doorstep sat a giant woman. It was almost night, and Jack went up to the giantess and said very politely, "Good-evening, ma'am. Would you be so kind as to give me some supper?"

"Is it supper you want?" said the big woman.
"It's supper you'll be if you don't move away
from here. My man is a giant, and he likes to
eat little boys."

"But I am very hungry," said Jack, "and
I've had no food at all this day since early
morning."

"Well, well," said the giantess, "I don't wonder
you are hungry, then. Come along to the kitchen
and I'll see what I can find for you."

So the giant's wife took Jack into the kitchen
and gave him a piece of cheese and a bowl of
bread and milk. He had not quite finished eating when, tramp! tramp! tramp! he heard the
steps of some one coming, and the whole castle
trembled with the heavy footfalls.

"Gracious me!" exclaimed the giant's wife,
"that's my man. Be quick now and jump into
the oven or he'll catch you;" and she bundled
Jack into the oven just as the giant came in.

The giant looked around the room and sniffed
the air. "Fe-fi-fo-fum, I smell fresh meat!"
said he.

"Yes," his wife responded, "the crows brought
a piece of raw flesh to-day to the top of the house
and dropped it on the roof."

"Ha!" said the giant, "I thought it was something nearer and fresher than that;" but he sat
down at the table and Jack watched him through
a crevice of the oven door, and was amazed to
see the quantity of food that he ate.

After supper was done the giant's wife cleared
away the dishes and went off to bed. "I am
getting a bit sleepy myself," said the giant; "but
I must have a look at my money," and he went
to a big chest and took out several bags full of

gold coins and returned to the table. He sat down and began to empty the bags one by one and was counting his wealth when he nodded off into a nap, and was soon snoring with a noise like thunder.

Jack then climbed out of the oven, and by getting on a chair beside the table he reached one of the bags of gold, and off he ran with it. As soon as he came to the bean-stalk he called out, " Hump it and bump it and down I go," and in a little while he was at the foot of the bean-stalk in his mother's garden.

Then he hurried to the house. There was a light in the window, and his mother was waiting for him in great anxiety, and was overjoyed to have him safely back.

They had money enough now, but Jack could not help thinking how many things the giant had which were rightfully theirs, and it was not long before he again climbed the bean-stalk. This time he carried some food, so that he did not have to beg of the giant's wife, and when he came to the great castle he got behind a rock and watched until he saw the giantess come out to the well with a pail after water. While she was busy at the well he ran into the kitchen and hid in a closet.

In a little while the woman brought in the pail of water, and by and by, tramp! tramp! came the giant. He began to sniff as soon as he entered the kitchen. "Fe-fi-fo-fum! I smell fresh meat!" he said.

"Do you?" said his wife. "Supposing we look around, then. If there's anybody hiding here it's likely to be in the oven."

So they both went to the oven, but luckily Jack was not there. "Well," said the giant's wife, "it's empty, and I thought it would be, and I'm tired of hearing your fe-fi-fo-fum!"

The giant wanted to look farther, but his wife said, "No, I won't have you mussing up the house. I know just how you would do it. You would turn everything that you could lay your hands on topsy-turvy. Besides, your supper is ready."

So the giant sat down and had his supper. After he had eaten, he said, "Wife, bring me the hen that lays the golden eggs."

She brought the hen and put it on the table. "If you don't need me any more, my dearie," said she, "I will go to the next room to finish some sewing I have there."

"No, I don't need you," replied the giant, "go

along." Then he took the little hen, and said, "Lay;" and the hen laid an egg of solid gold.

The giant took the egg in his hand, and looked at it for a while; but pretty soon he fell asleep and snored so that the house shook. Then Jack crept out of the closet and climbed on a chair by the table and grabbed the little hen and ran. That frightened the hen, and it gave a cackle which woke the giant. He sat up and rubbed his eyes, and Jack, who was now out of the door, heard him calling, "Wife, wife, what have you done with my golden hen?"

Jack heard her come hurrying to the kitchen from the next room and asking, "Why, my dear?"

But Jack kept running, and he got too far away to hear any more. In a short time he came to the bean-stalk, and shouted, "Hump it and bump it and down I go!" and soon he was at the foot of the bean-stalk and went into the house to his mother.

They took the best of care of the hen, and every day Jack told it to lay, and it laid a golden egg. But after a time Jack went up the bean-stalk again, and he kept going up every few days, until he had carried off pretty much all that the giant had. Finally, one night he tried to get the giant's bed-quilt. The quilt was made of silk of many colors, and it had beautiful jewels on it, and all along the edge were little silver bells that went tinkle, tinkle when Jack began to pull it.

The giant heard the bells and called out, " Who's round my house this dark, dismal night? "

Jack kept perfectly still until the giant was snoring, and then he pulled the quilt off a little farther. The bells went tinkle, tinkle, and the giant woke up and called out, " Who's round my house this dark, dismal night? "

So Jack stopped pulling and stayed as quiet as a mouse; but every time the giant fell asleep Jack got the bed-quilt a little farther off, till at last he had it all, and ran away with it. However, the bells made such a jingling as Jack ran that the giant was roused from his sleep and jumped up and started after him. Jack ran very swiftly, and got to the bean-stalk first. " Hump it and bump it and down I go," he shouted, and it did not take him long to get to his mother's garden.

But the giant was climbing down the bean-stalk after him, and the bean-stalk was shaking beneath the monster's weight. Jack could hear the giant

coming, and when he looked
up he saw the giant's legs just
appearing through the clouds.
Then Jack hurried to the
woodshed and got a hatchet
and began to chop at the bean-
stalk. The giant felt the bean-
stalk quiver, and stopped to
look down to find out
what was the matter.
Just at that moment
Jack gave a blow
with his hatchet that
brought bean-stalk,
giant, and all tum-
bling to the earth, and
that was the end of
the wicked giant.

As for Jack and
his mother, they were
rich people after that.

THE TWO BROTHERS AND
THE OLD WITCH

ONCE upon a time there were two boys who were brothers, and they were very poor. At last the older boy said, " I will go out into the world and try to make my fortune."

So he left his home, and he travelled about the world looking for work a long time. Finally, he reached a house in which an old witch woman lived, and she said she would give him work and pay him well.

" What shall I have to do ? " the boy asked.

" You must take care of my garden," said she, " and mow my meadow, and cut my wood, and once a week you must clean my fireplace; but I warn you never to look up the chimney."

The boy agreed to this bargain, and for many months he cared for the old woman's garden, and mowed her meadow, and cut her wood, and cleaned her fireplace. He liked his situation well enough, except that the old woman did not pay him his

wages.   Whenever he asked her for money she said,
"If you had it you would spend it.   No, no, I am
laying up what is due you in a stout leather bag

safely stowed away, and when you get to be as old
as I am you can have it."

This did not suit the boy, but he kept on with
his work until one day, as he was cleaning the fireplace, he heard a noise in the chimney, and he
looked up.   Immediately something heavy fell

whack on his head, bringing with it a lot of soot
that half blinded him.   As soon as he could get
the soot out of his eyes he saw on the hearth a
slender leather bag, and when he picked it up he
found it was full of money.   "This must be my
wages," said he, and he walked out of the door,
carrying the bag, and started off along the road
toward home.

By and by he came to a meeting-house, and the
meeting-house said, " Wait, wait, my lad, and sweep
me !   I have not been swept for seven long years."

But the boy said,

> "I'm in a hurry and cannot stay ;
> Perhaps I'll stop some other day."

He hastened on, and by and by he came to a
weedy field, and the field said, " Wait, wait, my lad,
and weed me.   I have not been weeded for seven
long years."

But the boy said,

> "I'm in a hurry and cannot stay ;
> Perhaps I'll stop some other day."

He hastened on, and by and by he came to a
cow, and the cow said, " Wait, wait, my lad, and
milk me.   I have not been milked for seven long
years."

But the boy said,

> " I 'm in a hurry and cannot stay ;
> Perhaps I 'll stop some other day."

He hastened on, and by and by he came to a well, and the well said, "Wait, wait, my lad, and clean me. I have not been cleaned for seven long years."
But the boy said,

> " I 'm in a hurry and cannot stay ;
> Perhaps I 'll stop some other day."

He hastened on, and by and by he came to an apple-tree so loaded with fruit that its branches were breaking down, and the tree said, "Wait, wait, my lad, and shake me. The apples you see on me have been growing for seven long years, and no one has come to shake them off or pick them."
But the boy said,

> " I 'm in a hurry and cannot stay ;
> Perhaps I 'll stop some other day."

However, instead of keeping on he sat down under the tree, and began to count his money.

Some time after he left the house where he had been working the old witch woman came in and saw the soot scattered about the fireplace. She looked up the chimney and discovered that her bag of money was gone. " That boy has taken it," she cried, " and I must catch him."

So she started in pursuit, and by and by she came to the meeting-house and said, -

> " Meeting-house, meeting-house,
> Have you seen a boy
> With a willy-willy wag
> And a long leather bag,
> Who 's stolen all the money
> That ever I had ? "

"Yes," replied the meeting-house, " he has gone on down the road."

So the witch went along until she came to a weedy field.   Then she said,

> ' Field of mine, field of mine,
> Have you seen a boy
> With a willy-willy wag
> And a long leather bag,
> Who 's stolen all the money
> That ever I had ? "

" Yes," replied the field, " he has gone on down the road."

So the witch went along until she came to a cow. Then she said,

> " Cow of mine, cow of mine,
> Have you seen a boy
> With a willy-willy wag
> And a long leather bag,
> Who 's stolen all the money
> That ever I had ? "

"Yes," replied the cow, "he has gone on down the road."

So the witch went along until she came to a well. Then she said,

> " Well of mine, well of mine.
> Have you seen a boy
> With a willy-willy wag
> And a long leather bag,
> Who 's stolen all the money
> That ever I had ? "

"Yes," replied the well, "he has gone on down the road."

So the witch went along until she approached the apple-tree, under which the boy was sitting counting his money. But he saw her coming, and he climbed the tree to hide among the branches. As soon as the witch was near enough she said,

> " Tree of mine, tree of mine,
> Have you seen a boy
> With a willy-willy wag
> And a long leather bag,
> Who 's stolen all the money
> That ever I had ? "

"Yes," was the tree's reponse, "he 's up here among my branches."

· Then the old woman pulled the boy out of the tree and gave him a sound beating, and he went away crying; while she took the bag of money and returned home.

A year or two after the first brother left to seek his fortune the other brother also started out into the world. He travelled about here and there and everywhere, looking for work and finding none. But, finally, he reached the house of the old witch woman, and she said she would give him work and pay him well.

"What shall I have to do?" the boy asked.

"You must take care of my garden," said she, "and mow my meadow, and cut my wood, and once a week you must clean my fireplace; but I warn you never to look up the chimney."

The boy agreed to this bargain, and for many months he cared for the old woman's garden, and mowed her meadow, and cut her wood, and cleaned her fireplace. He liked his situation well enough, except that the old woman did not pay him his wages. Whenever he asked her for money she said, "If you had it you would spend it. No, no, I am laying up what is due you in a stout leather bag stowed safely away, and when you get to be as old as I am you can have it."

This did not suit the boy, but he kept on with his work until one day, as he was cleaning the fire-

place, he heard a noise in the chimney and he
looked up. Immediately something heavy fell
whack on his head, bringing with it a lot of soot
that half blinded him. As soon as he could get
the soot out of his eyes he saw on the hearth a
slender leather bag, and when he picked it up he
found it was full of money. "This must be my
wages," said he, and he walked out of the door,
carrying the bag, and started off along the road
toward home.

By and by he came to a meeting-house, and
the meeting-house said, "Wait, wait, my lad, and
sweep me! I have not been swept for seven long
years!"

It was a large meeting-house, and he knew the
sweeping would be a hard task. However, he
stopped and swept the building very thoroughly.

Then he went on, and by and by he came to a
weedy field, and the field said, "Wait, wait, my
lad, and weed me! I have not been weeded for
seven long years."

It was a large field, and he knew the work would
be far from easy. However, he stopped and weeded
the whole field.

Then he went on, and by and by he came to a
cow, and the cow said, "Wait, wait, my lad, and

milk me! I have not been milked for seven long years."

The boy was in a hurry, but he stopped and milked the cow.

Then he went on, and by and by he came to a well, and the well said, "Wait, wait, my lad, and clean me! I have not been cleaned for seven long years."

The boy was in a hurry, but he stopped and cleaned the well.

Then he went on, and by and by he came to an apple-tree so loaded with fruit that its branches were breaking down, and the tree said, "Wait, wait, my lad, and shake me! The apples you see on me have been growing for seven long years, and no one has come to shake them off or pick them."

The boy was sorry for the tree, and he shook off enough of the apples, so that the branches were no longer in danger of breaking. "Thank you," said the tree; "now I can move my branches and shake off the rest myself when I choose."

The boy then sat down under the tree to count his money.

Some time after he left the house where he had been working the old witch woman came in and saw the soot scattered about the fireplace. She looked up the chimney and discovered that her bag of money was gone. " That boy has taken it," she cried, " and I must catch him."

So she started in pursuit, and by and by she came to a meeting-house and said,

> " Meeting-house, meeting-house,
>   Have you seen a boy
>   With a willy-willy wag
>   And a long leather bag,
>   Who 's stolen all the money
>   That ever I had ? "

But the meeting-house would not reply, and it loosened some of its shingles, and let them slide down onto the old woman, and she was glad to get away.

Then she went along until she came to what had been the weedy field, and she said,

> " Field of mine, field of mine,
>   Have you seen a boy
>   With a willy-willy wag
>   And a long leather bag,
>   Who 's stolen all the money
>   That ever I had ? "

But the field would not reply, and it raised a great cloud of dust and let it blow around the old witch, so that she was glad to get away.

Then she went along until she came to a cow, and she said,

> " Cow of mine, cow of mine,
>   Have you seen a boy
>   With a willy-willy wag
>   And a long leather bag,
>   Who 's stolen all the money
>   That ever I had ? "

But the cow would not reply, and it shook its horns at the old woman and frightened her, so that she was glad to get away.

Then she went along until she came to a well, and she said,

> " Well of mine, well of mine,
>   Have you seen a boy
>   With a willy-willy wag
>   And a long leather bag,
>   Who 's stolen all the money
>   That ever I had ? "

But the well would not reply, and it caused its water to rise and overflow, so that the old witch would have been drowned if she had not hastened to get away.

Then she went along until she approached the apple-tree, under which the boy was sitting counting his money. But he saw her coming, and he said,

> " Apple-tree, apple-tree, hide me,
>   So the old witch can't find me ! "

"Climb up among my branches and I will hide you," said the tree.

The boy climbed up, and the tree hid him with its leaves.   Pretty soon the old woman came and said,

"Tree of mine, tree of mine,
Have you seen a boy
With a willy-willy wag
And a long leather bag,
Who's stolen all the money
That ever I had?"

But the tree would not reply, and it shook its apples down on the old witch till she was glad to get away. She never found the boy, and he went home with the leather bag full of money, and after that he always prospered.

THE OLD WOMAN AND HER PIG

ONCE an old woman was sweeping her house and she found a piece of money, and she took the money to market and bought a pig. Then she told the pig to run home, and the pig said, "I won't!"

So the old woman looked around and she saw a dog, and she said, " Dog, dog, bite pig and make piggy run home. I see by the moonlight 't is half-past midnight — time pig and I were at home an hour ago."

But the dog said, "No, pig does n't do me any harm;" and he would n't.

So the old woman looked around and she saw a stick, and she said, "Stick, stick, bang dog, dog won't bite pig, and piggy won't run home. I see by the moonlight 't is half-past midnight — time pig and I were at home an hour ago."

But the stick said, "No, dog does n't do me any harm;" and it would n't.

So the old woman looked around and she saw a fire, and she said, " Fire, fire, burn stick, stick won't bang dog, dog won't bite pig, and piggy won't run home. I see by the moonlight 't is half-past midnight — time pig and I were at home an hour ago."

But the fire said, " No, stick does n't do me any harm ;" and it would n't.

So the old woman looked around and she saw a puddle of water, and she said, " Water, water, quench fire, fire won't burn stick, stick won't bang dog, dog won't bite pig, and piggy won't run home. I see by the moonlight 't is half-past midnight — time pig and I were at home an hour ago."

. But the water said, " No, fire does n't do me any. harm ;" and it would n't.

So ·the old woman looked around and she saw an ox, and she said, " Ox, ox, drink water, water won't quench fire, fire won't burn stick, stick won't bang dog, dog won't bite pig, and piggy won't run home. I see by the moonlight 't is half-past midnight — time pig and I were at home an hour ago."

But the ox said, " No, water does n't do me any harm ;" and it would n't.

LADY FEATHERFLIGHT

ONCE there was a poor woman who had a son named Jack, and they lived on the edge of a wood. Times were hard, and they did not always have enough to eat, and at last the woman said to her son, " Jack, you must now go out into the wide world; for if you stay here we shall both starve. We have only half a loaf of bread left, but you shall take that with you, and I wish it were larger. The world lies on the other side of the forest. Find your way to it and gain your living honestly."

So she bade Jack good-by, and he started. On he went, farther and farther into the forest, and he walked all day and saw no farm or dwelling or path. Then he knew that he was lost, but he kept on as long as daylight lasted, and when it became dark he lay down and slept. During the day he had eaten nearly all of his bread, and the next morning he ate what was left and wandered on again through the trackless woods until evening. Night came, and he was looking for a spot where he could lie down and sleep when he saw lights before him. So he went toward the lights and presently came to a large palace. He knocked at the entrance and a beautiful young woman opened the door.

"My good lady," said Jack, "I have been lost for two days in this great forest, and I beg that you will give me something to eat."

"No, no," said she, "go away as quickly as you can. The owner of this palace is a giant. He will soon come home and he will surely eat you."

"Can't you hide me?" asked Jack. "Unless I have food and shelter I shall die."

"I could not hide you so but that he would find you," said she. "Oh, do go away at once!"

"Perhaps he would not eat me," argued Jack. "He has not eaten you."

"That is because he wants me to take care of his house and cook his food," said she; "but I do not know how soon he will change his mind. Please, sir, hurry away, or it will be too late."

However, Jack insisted that rather than starve in the forest he would risk death at the hands of the giant. So finally she yielded and allowed him to enter, and when she had given him something to eat hid him in a cupboard beside the fireplace.

After a while the giant came banging at the door, shouting, "Featherflight, let me in, let me in!"

She unlocked the door, and as he came tramping into the room he said, "Where's that man? I began to smell him ten miles away as I was coming through the woods."

"Don't you think you were mistaken?" asked Featherflight.

But the giant did not reply. He sniffed the air for a moment and then went to the cupboard beside the fireplace and pulled Jack out.

"Did you mean him?" said Featherflight. "Why, that is nothing but a poor, thin, little fellow who would scarcely make you half a mouthful, and his bones would stick in your throat. Would n't it be better to keep him and make him work for you? But your supper is ready now, and you can think about what to do with him afterward."

So she set before the giant a vast quantity of meat and drink, and he ate so much and gobbled it down so fast that the sight made Jack's hair stand on end as he stood watching him. When the giant had finished, he looked at Jack scorn-

fully and remarked, " Ah, it is as Featherflight
said — you are only half a mouthful; but there is

room for flesh on your bones, and we shall have
to fatten you.   Meanwhile, you must earn your
victuals.   See here, my young snip, can you do
a day's work in a day?"

"Yes," answered Jack bravely, "I can do a day's work in a day as well as another."

So the giant said, "Well, go to bed now. I will tell you what your work shall be in the morning."

Jack went to bed, and early the next day the giant took him out to the farmyard and showed him a large barn from the roof of which a recent storm had blown off the thatch. "Behind this barn," said the giant, "you will find a great heap of feathers. Thatch me this barn with those feathers, and if the job is not done by the time I come back to-night, I shall eat you at once, without waiting for you to get any fatter."

Then he left, laughing as he went; for he thought he had given Jack a job he could not possibly do.

Jack found a ladder and a basket and began work. He filled the basket and climbed the ladder, and tried hard to lay and fasten the feathers in place on the roof, but the wind would catch them and scatter them far and wide. He kept at his task for hours, and the heap of feathers was half gone. Yet he had only succeeded in thatching a narrow strip along one edge of the roof. Finally, he sat down at the foot of the ladder, completely discouraged. Pretty soon Lady Featherflight came with some food for him, and he told her his troubles.

"Well," said she, "while you are eating I will see what I can do to help you."

Then she began walking around the barn, singing as she went, ·

> "Birds of land and birds of sea,
> Come and thatch this roof for me."

She was walking around the second time when the sky grew dark with what seemed like a heavy cloud that hid the sun. The cloud came nearer and nearer to the earth, and at length proved to be made of hundreds and thousands of birds. They came directly to the barn, and each alighted on the roof with a feather in its beak, and after tucking the feather neatly in flew away. Thus by the time Jack's meal was finished the roof was finished, too.

Then Featherflight said, "Now let us talk and enjoy ourselves until the giant comes home."

So they walked about the garden and grounds, and Jack thought those hours were the pleasantest he had ever known in his life. Toward evening they went into the house and Jack helped Featherflight prepare the giant's supper, which consisted of fourteen loaves of bread, two sheep roasted whole, and a ·pudding you could not have put in a bushel basket.

By and by the giant came back and pounded at the door with his fists, shouting, " Let me in, let me in ! "

As soon as he entered he called to Jack and asked how he had got on with his thatching.

" You 'll have no fault to find," said Jack. " I told you I could do a day's work in a day as well as another, and I can."

The giant made no response, but sat down and ate his supper. The next morning he had Jack go out with him while he looked at the barn roof. " I know very well that was not your doing," he remarked.

Then he went on a little beyond the barn and showed Jack a vast heap of grain seeds of many different kinds. " Here is your day's work," said he. '' Separate the seeds each into its own pile, and if the job is n't done by the time I come back to-night I shall eat you at once, without fail."

So saying he left, laughing to himself as he went.

Jack sat down before the heap, took a handful of seeds, put wheat in one pile, rye in another,

barley in another, and oats in another.   But though
he worked very industriously, the great heap was
scarcely diminished at all when noon came.   Jack
was tired out, and he sat down with his back against
the foundation wall of the barn, feeling very sorrowful.   Pretty soon Featherflight came with some
food for him, and he told her how badly he was
getting along with his day's task.

" Well," said she, " while you are eating I will
see what I can do to help you."

Then she began walking around the heap of
seeds, singing as she went,

> " Little insects, far and near,
>   Come and sort the seeds heaped here."

She was walking around the heap the second
time when the ground all about appeared as if it
were moving.   From behind each lump of earth,
each daisy stem and blade of grass, there came
some little insect, gray, black, brown, or green, and
began to work at the seeds; and there was such
a multitude of insects that by the time Jack's
meal was finished the sorting was done.

For the rest of the day Jack and Lady Featherflight walked and talked in the garden to their
hearts' content.   With the approach of evening
they went into the palace, and Jack helped get

supper, and then the giant came thumping at the door, and shouting, "Let me in, let me in!"

As soon as Featherflight opened the door the giant called to Jack to know how he had succeeded with his seed-sorting.

"You'll have no fault to find," said Jack; "for I spoke only the truth when I told you I could do a day's work in a day as well as another."

Then the giant sat down and ate with a great appetite four fat pigs, three hens and a gander, finishing off with a monster pudding. After he had disposed of these things he was so sleepy he could not hold his head up, and he said to Jack, "Go to bed, youngster; I'll see your work to-morrow."

In the morning he called Jack early out to the farmyard, and looked at the seeds. "You never did that sorting alone," said he.

Then he walked on a little farther and showed Jack a heap of sand and said, "From this sand you must make me a hundred ropes with which I may tether my herd of cows, and if the job is not done by the time I am back to-night I shall eat you immediately."

So saying he turned on his heel and went away laughing.

Jack took some sand into his hands to see if he could by any means twist it into the form of a rope.   But his efforts were wasted, and he threw the sand away and went into the palace to tell Featherflight how things were.   " I know you would help me if you could," said he ; " but this task is beyond you, and I feel myself between the giant's teeth already."

" Don't be so disheartened," she responded. " Sit down and we will plan what to do."

They talked and planned all the day until at last they had to stop to get the giant's supper ready.   At length the giant came slamming at the door, and he was no sooner in than he wanted to know how Jack had got along with his rope-making.

" It is as I told you," replied Jack ; " I can do a day's work in a day as well as another, and you are welcome to see what I have done in the morning."

Then the giant sat down and ate heartily and went off to bed.   But Jack and Lady Feather-flight waited in the kitchen until they heard the giant snoring, and then Featherflight took the keys of the treasure-room and they went together and got several bags of gold.   After that they hurried out and selected the best horse in the best stable, and Jack mounted with Featherflight behind him and off they went.

At three o'clock the next morning the giant woke and called out, "Jack, get up;" for Jack's room was near by, and the giant's command would certainly have been heard had Jack been in his room as the giant supposed.

But there was no response, and the giant turned over and went to sleep. At four o'clock the giant woke again and called out, "*Jack, get up!*"

But he received no reply, and he turned over and went to sleep. At five o'clock he awoke the third time and shouted, "JACK, GET UP!"

"What ails the fellow?" he growled when he received no answer. "I'll rouse him out in a way he won't like," and the giant went stamping along the passage.

Of course Jack's room was empty, and after the giant had looked in and noticed that the bed had not been slept in he went downstairs to the kitchen. Everything was cold and silent there — no fire, no Jack, no Featherflight. "Ah, ha!" he exclaimed, "they've like enough run away."

Then he hastened out to the farmyard and found the door of his best stable open and his best horse gone. But the giant was so big and strong that he could outrun any horse in the world, and he went after Jack and Featherflight as swift as the wind. They had been galloping all the night, but now the day was come and presently Jack heard a sound behind them, and turning to look he saw the giant striding along to catch them. "Oh, Featherflight," he cried, "all is lost!"

But Featherflight said, "Keep steady, Jack, let the horse go right on."

Then she took from her pocket a little stick and threw it back over her left shoulder. Immediately there grew up behind them a hard-wood forest so dense and tangled the giant could not get through it.

"We are saved," said Jack.

"That's not so certain," responded Featherflight; "but at any rate we have gained some time."

The giant was obliged to go home to get an ax. However, he quickly returned and hacked and hewed his way through the woods and was on the trail again. Presently Jack heard him coming. "Oh, Featherflight," he said, "there is the giant! He will soon overtake us. We cannot escape him this time."

*The magic forest stops the giant in his pursuit of Jack and
Lady Featherflight*

`"Keep steady, Jack," she said, "and let the horse go straight on."

Then she took from her pocket a little vial of water and threw it back over her right shoulder, and the vial broke when it fell to the ground, and the water became a deep lake between them and the giant. Jack was so elated then that he stopped the horse and waved his hat toward the giant who was standing on the farther shore.

The giant shook his fist at them and looked this way and that, in doubt what to do next. "How can I get over?" the monster bellowed.

"Drink your way through," shouted Jack.

So the giant stooped down and drank and drank and drank until he burst, and that was the end of him.

As for Jack and Featherflight, they went on now more leisurely, for they no longer feared pursuit. By and by they came near to a town and stopped under a tree. "Featherflight," said Jack, "you climb this tree and hide, and I will go to the town to get a parson to come and marry us. Another thing I must do is to buy a suit of fine clothes before I am seen with so beautiful a lady as yourself."

So Featherflight climbed the tree and hid in the

thick leafage. She found a comfortable place to sit among the branches, and then she observed that directly below her was a clear spring into which she could look and see the reflection of her face as in a mirror. This spring was used by all the housewives of the town, and every morn and noon and evening they resorted thither to gossip and fill their pails and pitchers. No water was so sweet anywhere else. Featherflight had not been long in the tree when the carpenter's wife came and bent over the spring. There she saw Featherflight's lovely face reflected; but she thought it was her own and she looked with astonishment, exclaiming, "What! I a carpenter's wife and so handsome; and here I am a common drudge come to this spring for water. Well, I'll do no more such work! I'll go away from this poor little town and seek my fortune."

So she threw down her pitcher, and off she went along the road that led away from the town.

The next woman who came for water was the butcher's wife, and as she bent over the clear spring she saw Featherflight's lovely face; but she thought it was her own. She gazed with astonishment, exclaiming, "What! I a butcher's wife and so handsome ; yet here I am a common drudge. Well, I 'll do no more housework ! I 'll leave this poor little town at once and seek my fortune."

So she threw down the pail she had in her hand, and off she went along the road that led away from the town.

In the same manner all the other wives of the town came and looked in the spring and were surprised at what they thought was their own beauty and went away to seek their fortunes.

But presently the men of the town began to want their dinners, and one by one they went out on the streets each to ask the others if they had by any chance seen his wife. No, not a wife had been seen since they had gone for water. Then the men began to fear foul play, and all together they walked out of the town to the spring. When they reached it they found many broken pitchers and overturned pails strewn around, and were certain then their wives had met with some mysterious disaster. One of the men happened to glance into the spring and saw a face reflected. He knew it was not his own, and he began to look about. In a moment or two he saw Lady Featherflight among the branches of the tree, and he called to his comrades, " Here is some one in the tree. I'll wager she knows what has become of our wives, and has had something to do with spiriting them away."

"Yes!" cried another. "Here is the enchantress. She has bewitched our wives. Let us kill her!"

They began to drag her out of the tree in spite of all she could say or do; but just then Jack came galloping back on his horse with the parson mounted behind; and in his fine new clothes you would hardly have known him to be the poor ragged fellow who passed over the road in the other direction only a short time previous. As he drew near he saw the crowd and shouted, "What's the matter? What are you doing with that lady?"

The men replied, "We are going to hang her. She has bewitched our wives, and murdered them, too, for all we know."

Then the parson got down off the horse from behind Jack and told the men to stop and let Lady Featherflight tell her own story. So they asked her what she had to say for herself, and when she told them how their wives had mistaken her face in the spring for theirs and what the wives had said they were silent for a few moments, and then one and all exclaimed, "Well, if that is what our wives think of themselves we will seek for them no farther. They can come home when they get ready;" and the men turned and walked back to the town.

The parson married Jack and Lady Featherflight on the spot, and then they also went to the town, and there they saw a splendid mansion they thought they would like and Jack bought it. In that they lived happily for many months, but at last Jack began to wish for more of the giant's treasure and proposed that they should go back after it. "But how could we cross the lake you made?" said he.

"We might build a bridge," replied Lady Featherflight.

The bridge was built and they went over it with many wagons and horses, and loaded the wagons at the giant's palace with great riches. But as the wagons on their return were crossing the bridge the last one broke the bridge down, and all the gold and silver and jewels on that wagon were lost in the lake.

"Alas!" Jack lamented, "now the bridge is gone and we can get nothing more from the giant's treasure-room."

6

But Lady Featherflight said, "Why not mend the bridge?"

"To be sure!" said Jack, "why not?"

> So the bridge was mended
> And my story's ended.

THE LITTLE RED HEN AND THE WHEAT

ONCE there was a little red hen, and she found a grain of wheat in the barnyard and said, " Who will plant this wheat ? "

" I won't," says the dog.

" I won't," says the cat.

" I won't," says the goose.

" I won't," says the turkey.

" I will, then," says the little red hen. " Ca-ca-ca-ca-ca-ca-ca-ca-*daa*-cut ! "

So she planted the grain of wheat. Pretty soon the wheat began to grow and the green leaves came up out of the ground. The sun shone and the rain fell and the wheat kept on growing until it was a tall, strong stalk and had a big head of ripe grain at the top.

" Who will reap this wheat ? " says the little red hen.

" I won't," says the dog.

" I won't," says the cat.

"I won't," says the goose.

"I won't," says the turkey.

"I will, then," says the little red hen.   "Ca-ca-ca-ca-ca-ca-ca-*daa*-cut!"

So she reaped the wheat.

"Who will thresh this wheat?" says the little red hen.

"I won't," says the dog.

"I won't," says the cat.

"I won't," says the goose.

"I won't," says the turkey.

"I will, then," says the little red hen.   "Ca-ca-ca-ca-ca-ca-ca-*daa*-cut!"

So she threshed the wheat.

"Who will take this wheat to mill to have it ground?" says the little red hen.

"I won't," says the dog.

"I won't," says the cat.

"I won't," says the goose.

"I won't," says the turkey.

'I will, then," says the little red hen.   "Ca-ca-ca-ca-ca-ca-ca-*daa*-cut!"

So she took the wheat to mill, and by and by she came back with the flour.

"Who will bake this flour?" says the little red hen.

"I won't," says the dog.

"I won't," says the cat.

"I won't," says the goose.

"I won't," says the turkey.

"I will, then," says the little red hen. "Ca-ca-ca-ca-ca-ca-ca-ca-*daa*-cut!"

So she baked the flour and made a loaf of bread.

"Who will eat this bread?" says the little red hen.

"I will," says the dog.

"I will," says the cat.

"I will," says the goose.

"I will," says the turkey.

"*I* will," says the little red hen. "Ca-ca-ca-ca-ca-ca-ca-ca-*daa*-cut!" and she ate the loaf of bread all up.

A BEAR STORY

AS I was going up stin-dum-stair-um I met a high-gig-gle-y-bon-bear-um carrying off my fin-dum-fair-um ; and I said, " I wish I had my gish-me-gair-um ; I 'd show that high-gig-gle-y-bon-bear-um how to carry off my fin-dum-fair-um ! "

In plain English this nursery tale is as follows :

As I was going up stairs I met a bear carry-ing off my hog ; and I said, " I wish I had my gun ; I 'd show that bear how to carry off my hog ! "

FOOLISH JIM AND CLEVER JAMES

THERE was once a fellow who was so simple that people called him Foolish Jim. Every one made fun of him, for he would keep a candle burning all through the day, and when it began to be dark he would blow the light out. He would carry an umbrella spread over his head to protect himself from the rain when there was not a cloud in the sky. He would wear an overcoat on the hottest day of summer and walk about outdoors in his shirt sleeves in midwinter. Indeed, he did everything contrary to common sense. By and by the king heard of him, and, thinking Foolish Jim would afford some amusement, he sent for him. When Jim came he looked so awkward that the king and all his courtiers began to laugh.

"Do you know how to count?" asked the king.

"I know how to count eggs," Foolish Jim replied, "for yesterday I found four and two."

"How many does that make?" said the king.

"I can't say," Jim answered, "but I will go and count the eggs and find out."

"Very well," said the king.

So Foolish Jim went and counted the eggs, and when he returned he told the king there were four and two.

The king and his friends made merry over this response for some time, but at last the king said, "How would you like to marry my daughter, Foolish Jim?"

"That would just suit me," Jim replied.

"All right," said the king; "then I must explain to you that about a month ago I agreed my daughter should marry the first man who guessed a riddle that I have made. I allow three guesses, and whoever tries the three times and fails is put to death. Fifty men have lost their lives already. So take warning and remember that you need not try unless you choose."

"Oh, yes! I will try," said Jim. "Let me hear the riddle."

"The riddle is this," responded the king. "What is it that early in the morning walks on four legs, at noon on two, and in the evening on three legs? You may come again on the first day of April and answer me."

So Jim went away, and he did nothing but think until the first of April came. Every one knew that he was going to try to guess the king's riddle, and they all thought he would surely fail. Most of them were sorry for him, and the only person who was glad was a bad man who was one of Jim's neighbors. This man wanted to have Jim's horse, and he said to himself, " Jim is so foolish there is no chance whatever of his guessing that riddle. I may as well save him the trouble of going to the king, and at the same time get his horse for my own."

The first day of April came, and the bad man put a basket of poisoned cakes on a bridge over which Foolish Jim was to pass. " He will eat those cakes," said the man, "and then he will die and I will take the horse."

Pretty soon Foolish Jim came riding along, and when he saw the basket of cakes on the bridge he got off his horse and picked them up. " This is very queer," said he; "a basket of cakes and no one in sight to whom they might belong."

They smelled good and were very tempting, but he was a little suspicious. " I will give a few of them to my horse before I eat any," said he.

So he took up several of the cakes and fed them to the horse, and almost immediately the poor beast fell dead on the bridge. "See," said Foolish Jim, "if I had not been prudent, it is I who would

be dead instead of my horse. Well, well, and now I shall have to go the rest of the way on foot."

Before he started he threw his horse into the river, and as the body was being carried away by the current three buzzards alighted on it and began to eat. Foolish Jim watched his horse until it floated around a turn in the river and disappeared. "Now," said he, wagging his head, "I shall have something to ask the king to guess."

When Foolish Jim arrived at the king's palace he found no rivals, for so many had failed and been beheaded that others who were inclined to have a try at the riddle were a good deal discouraged. But Jim went directly to the king and said, "If I guess your riddle, will you give me your daughter?"

"Yes," the king replied.

"Well, the riddle is easily answered," said Foolish Jim.

"Say no more," commanded the king, "but let us have the answer at once."

"Hearken, then," said Foolish Jim. "A little child before he is able to stand walks on four legs; when he grows stronger he walks on two, and when he is old he has to carry a cane and that makes three legs."

All persons present had been listening with their mouths wide open, they were so astonished.

"You have guessed right," said the king, "and I see you are not so foolish as you would have people believe. My daughter will be your wife."

"I beg you will allow me to ask *you* a riddle now," said Foolish Jim.

The king thought he was so keen at guessing riddles that it would be impossible to ask one he could not correctly answer. " Certainly," he replied, " and if I do not guess it I will forfeit my kingdom to you."

Then Foolish Jim said, " I saw a dead being that was carrying three living beings and was nourishing them. The dead did not touch the land and was not in the sky. Tell me what it was, or I shall take your kingdom."

The king tried to guess. He said this, that, and a thousand things ; but in the end he had to give up, and Foolish Jim said, " The dead being was my horse. He died on a bridge. I threw him into the river, and as he floated away three buzzards alighted on him and were eating him, and he did not touch the land and was not in the sky."

Everybody now saw that Foolish Jim was smarter than all of them together. He married the king's daughter and took the monarch's place and governed the kingdom, and instead of being called Foolish Jim he was known as " Clever James."

THE BEGGAR AND THE PRINCESS

ONCE there was a boy who had a wonderful horse. When he wanted to ride, all he had to do was to say, "Saddle and bridle my little horse," and no matter where the boy was the horse came immediately, all ready to be mounted.

Then the boy would go for a ride, and when he had ridden as much as he pleased, he would dismount and say, "Off saddle, off bridle," and at once in place of the horse there was a little cloud of mist that in a moment afterward had melted into nothing.

The boy lived with his mother, but at length he grew up, and was tired of staying at home. So he set out to seek adventures. He told no one where he was going, but mounted his horse and travelled for a long time until he arrived in the country of a great king. As he was riding through this country he came to a large city, and in the midst of the city lived the king in a handsome palace. The young man stopped his horse before the palace and sat admiring the fine building when a coach came forth from the gates and passed him. In the coach sat the king's daughter, and she was very beautiful.

"Ah!" said the young man, "I wish I might marry that beautiful princess. I must contrive some way to speak with her."

So he dismounted and said, "Off saddle, off bridle," and his horse was instantly gone from sight.

Now he went to a second-hand clothing shop in the city and bought the most ragged suit of clothes he could get, and after that he sought out a lodging-place for the night.

The next morning he dressed himself in the ragged clothes and put his other clothes in a bundle and returned to the king's palace. He went in at a side gate and around to the rear to the kitchen, and made signs that he wanted work. He would say no words, but only mumbled, and the king's servants thought he was an idiot. However, they were kind to him, and he helped them at their work and they let him sleep on the kitchen hearth. As they did not know his name they called him "The Beggar."

He remained in the kitchen for a whole week, and when Sunday came everybody in the palace went to church except the beggar and the princess. As to the beggar, no one thought of his going, for his clothes were not good enough; and the

princess stayed at home because she was not feeling well that day.

The rest of the household were no sooner out of the way than the beggar put on his fine garments, which he had kept tied up in a bundle, and said, "Saddle and bridle my little horse."

The horse appeared at once, and the young man began to ride back and forth on the paths of the palace gardens. Pretty soon the princess saw him and she stepped out on a little balcony and called to him to know who he was. So he came close up under the window, and they talked together until they heard the people coming from church. Then the young man dashed away to get out of sight, and in his haste ran his horse across a flower-bed and broke some of the pots and tender plants. But he got safely to the kitchen and made his horse disappear and put on his shabby clothes again.

The damage in the garden was reported to the king, and he tried to discover who had done it, and was very angry. He summoned his servants, but they said that the beggar was the only one who had remained at home. So the king questioned the beggar, but he would only mumble in reply, and the king could do nothing with him.

The next Sunday every one went to church except the princess and the beggar. She stayed at home because she wanted to see him again, and no one expected him to go because his clothes were not good enough. But when the other servants were gone it did not take him long to get into his fine garments and call for his horse. Then he rode in

the garden, and presently he saw the princess at her
window waiting to speak with him.

They talked together just as they had the week
before, until they heard the people coming from
church, and then the young man had to hurry to
get out of sight. There was no time to lose, and
he galloped across a flower-bed and broke some
more pots and tender plants.

The king was furious when he saw this new
damage, and he declared that the rascal who was
spoiling his garden must be caught.

So the third Sunday the king stayed at home from
church, and hid in the palace cellar where there was
a narrow window that looked out on the garden.
Thence he watched, and presently he saw the young
man riding on the paths, and he ran out and caught
the horse by the bridle.

"What do you mean, you villain, by riding
around in my garden this way?" shouted the king.
"I'll have your head taken off as soon as my
servants get back from church."

The young man leaped down from his horse and
said, "Off saddle, off bridle," and the king saw a
little puff of fog disappearing, and the horse was
gone, and his hand that had gripped the horse's
bridle was empty.

He rubbéd his eyes. "Good heavens!" he exclaimed, "can you do such things as that?"

"Yes," said the young man, "and I beg you will hear my story."

So he told the king all about himself and his wonderful horse, and the king was very much interested. Last of all the young man told the king how he loved his daughter, and that he wanted to marry her; and the king said he was willing. So the young man sent for his mother, and he married the princess, and they lived a long time and were very happy.

THE OGRE'S WIFE

ONCE upon a time there was a pretty young girl who was very proud, and she never failed to find some pretext or other for sending promptly away every young man who came to court her. One was too fat, another was too thin, this one had red hair, that one had big feet. In short she refused all her suitors.

Finally her mother picked a pumpkin and had it put on the top of a very tall pole. "Do you see that pumpkin?" said she to her daughter. "The young man who climbs up and gets that pumpkin will be your husband."

The daughter said she did not object; but her reason for not objecting was that she did not think any young man could climb so slender and lofty a pole. They sent notices far and wide and appointed a day for the climbers to show their agility. When the day came a crowd of young men presented themselves, and the last to arrive was handsomer and more beautifully dressed than

any of the others. He was an ogre in disguise, but
nobody knew him, and the young girl admired his
appearance so much that she said to her mother, " I
hope he will get the pumpkin."

One after another the young men tried to climb
the pole, and one after another they failed to climb
high enough to seize the pumpkin and had to
return to the ground without it. However, when
the turn of the ogre came he climbed with ease right
up to the top of the pole and brought the pumpkin
down with him. Then he said to the young girl,
" Come now, we will go home to my house."

The girl put on her best dress and got into the
ogre's carriage and went away with him. On the
road they met a man who said to the ogre, " Give
me my hat and gloves which I lent to you."

The ogre took off his hat and gloves and gave
them to the man. " Here, take your old hat and
gloves ! " said he, and drove on.

Pretty soon another man met them and said to
the ogre, " Give me my coat which I lent to you."

The ogre took off his coat and gave it to the man.
" Here, take your old coat ! " he said, and drove on.

After a while another man stopped them and
said to the ogre, " Give me my collar and cravat
which I lent to you."

The ogre took off his collar and cravat and gave
them to the man. " Here, take your old collar and
cravat ! " he said, and drove on.

He was not at all well dressed now, and the
young girl did not think he looked nearly so handsome as when she first saw him, and she was
beginning to be very much frightened. At last,
when they were almost to the ogre's house, another
man met them and said, " Give me my horses
which I lent to you."

The ogre gave him the two horses that drew
the carriage. " Here, take your old horses ! " he
said.

When the man was gone with the horses, the
ogre ordered his wife to get out and draw the
carriage the rest of the way. This she did, and she
was more scared than she had ever been before in
her life. Pretty soon they came to where the
ogre lived, and he said to his wife, " I shall be
away until evening. Go in and stay with my
housekeeper until I return."

She went indoors, and the housekeeper said,
" Ah, my dear, you have taken a bad husband.
You have married an ogre."

The poor girl was very much distressed when she
heard what he really was, and she said to the old

woman, "Could you not tell me how I can run away?"

"Yes, I will tell you," replied the old woman. "Go and hide in the chicken-house, and spend the night there. It is time now to give the chickens their evening feed. You will find a sack of corn just inside the door. Let them have all of the corn they will eat, especially the rooster. It is the rooster's business to awake his master in the morning, and if he has a full crop he will oversleep and give you a better chance to get away. Start as soon as you can see, and carry with you four eggs from the chicken-house nests. If you find the ogre chasing you, throw an egg on the ground behind you."

The young lady did all that the ogre's housekeeper told her to do, and in the earliest gray of the morning she left the chicken-house, carrying four eggs tied up in her handkerchief.

The ogre's rooster had eaten so much corn that he overslept and gave the girl a long start, but when he awoke he at once began to crow and make a great racket, shouting, "Master, master! get up quickly! Some one has run away! Cock-a-doodle-do!"

The ogre got up without delay and started at a tremendous pace after his wife. She presently saw him coming and dashed an egg on the ground behind her. Immediately there rose between her and her pursuer a high, strong wooden fence, and the ogre could neither get through it nor over it, and had to go home to get an ax to cut the fence down. But after a time he returned and chopped a passage for himself, and then went on faster than ever.

As soon as the girl saw him coming she threw back another egg, and there rose a brick wall so lofty the ogre could not climb over it, and he had to go home for a heavy hammer with which to break the wall down. But after a time he returned and smashed his way through, and then went on faster than ever.

The girl heard him coming and threw back another egg, and behind her burned a long line of fire, and the ogre had to go home for a jar of water to put out the fire. After a time he returned and with the water, quenched the fire, and then went on faster than ever.

When the girl heard him coming she threw her last egg; but in her haste she made a misthrow, and the egg, instead of falling behind her, fell in front of her, and immediately she found herself on the bank of a broad river that shut off farther flight. However, close by the shore she saw a big crocodile warming itself in the sun, and the girl said, "Grandmother, I pray you, cross me over. Grandmother, I pray you, save my life."

The crocodile replied, "Sit down on my back and I will cross you over."

So the girl sat down on the broad back of the crocodile and it swam swiftly out into the stream away from the ogre, and she escaped to the other side. Then the crocodile swam back, and the ogre said, "Cross me over, crocodile ; cross me over, too."

The crocodile replied, "Very well, sit down on my back."

The ogre sat down on the crocodile's back, and the crocodile swam toward the other shore, but when it reached the middle of the river it dived under the water and the ogre was drowned.

The girl had been carried safely over, and she climbed the bank and found an old black horse feeding in a pasture, and she said to it, "I pray you, horse, save my life."

"Well," said the horse, "get up on my back and I will carry you to your mother."

So the girl mounted the old black horse, and the horse carried her safely to her mother's house, and there she is still.

When the crocodile reached the middle of the river he dived

THE FOX AND THE LITTLE
RED HEN

ONCE upon a time there was a little red hen which lived in the edge of a piece of woodland.

On the other side of the woods dwelt a cunning robber fox with his mother, and one day the robber fox said, " Mother, you make a fire and get the pot boiling, for I 'm going to catch the little red hen and we 'll cook her as soon as I come back and have her for dinner."

So he slung a bag over his shoulder, and started for the little red hen's house.

The little red hen never suspected any danger, and she did her morning work as usual, and then looked at her clock to see what time it was. " Well," said she, " now I must begin to get dinner, and the first thing I 'll do is to step out into the yard for a few chips to make my fire burn more briskly."

So out she went, and while she was filling her apron with the chips the fox came along and slipped into the house without her seeing him, and hid behind the door. " I 'll catch her easily enough, now," said he.

Pretty soon the little red hen went in and was just going to shut and lock the door when she saw the fox. Then she was so frightened that she dropped all her chips and flew up to a peg in the wall.

" Ha, ha!" laughed the robber fox, "it won't take me long to bring you down from there;" and he began running round and round after his tail.

The little red hen kept turning about on the peg to watch him, and in a few minutes she got so dizzy that she fell off.

Then the fox picked her up, and put her in his bag, and started for home feeling very smart. But he grew tired by and by and sat down to rest; and the little red hen began to wonder if she could contrive to escape. She did not want to be eaten, and she thought and thought until she happened to think that she had her scissors in her pocket. She did not waste any more time, but took the scissors and snipped a hole in the bag and jumped out.

The ground just there was strewn with stones, and the little red hen picked up several as large as she could lift and put them in the bag in her place. Then she ran home as fast as she could go.

After a while the fox got up and went on. "How heavy this little hen is!" he said to himself.

"She must be very plump and fat. Ah! won't she make a good dinner!" and he smacked his lips to think of how nice she would taste.

When he came in sight of his house he saw his mother standing in the doorway watching for him, and he called out, "Hi, mother, have you got the pot boiling?"

"Yes, yes," his mother replied; "and have you got the little red hen?"

"She's here in this bag I have on my shoulder," was his answer, "and she'll make a fine dinner."

He was soon at the house and he and his mother went inside. "Now," said he, "when I count three you take the cover off the pot and I'll pop the little red hen right into the hot water."

"Very well," said his mother.

"All ready!" said the fox, "one, two, three!"

His mother took the cover off, and splash went the stones into the boiling water, and the pot tipped over and scalded the robber fox and his mother to death.

But the little red hen lives in the woods by herself yet.

THE HOBYAHS

ONCE there was an old man and an old woman and a little girl, and they all lived together in a house made of hempstalks, and they had a little dog named Turpie.

One night the Hobyahs came and said, "Hobyah! Hobyah! Hobyah! Tear down the hempstalks, eat up the old man and woman, and carry off the little girl!"

But little dog Turpie barked so that the Hobyahs all ran off; and the old man said, "Little dog

Turpie barks so that I cannot sleep nor slumber, and if I live till morning I will sell him."

So when it was morning the old man took little dog Turpie and was gone all day trying to sell him. "You can have him for four shillings," said he to every person he met; but no one would buy him. Some did not want a dog, others lacked money, and the old man had to bring little dog Turpie back home.

That night the Hobyahs came again and said, "Hobyah! Hobyah! Hobyah! Tear down the hempstalks, eat up the old man and woman, and carry off the little girl."

But little dog Turpie barked so that the Hobyahs all ran off; and the old man said, "Little dog

Turpie barks so that I cannot sleep nor slumber, and if I live till morning I will sell him."

So when it was morning the old man took little dog Turpie and was gone all day trying to sell him. "You can have him for three shillings," said he to

every person he met; but no one would buy him.
Some did not want a dog, and others did not have
the three shillings. The only man who wanted a
dog and had the money refused to buy when he
learned that the reason why Turpie's master wished
to sell him was because he barked so; and the old
man had to bring little dog Turpie back home.

That night the
Hobyahs
came again
and said,
" Hobyah!
Hobyah! Hobyah! Tear down the hempstalks,
eat up the old man and woman, and carry off the
little girl!"

But little dog Turpie barked so that the Hobyahs
all ran off; and the old man said, " Little dog

Turpie barks so that I cannot sleep nor slumber,
and if I live till morning I will sell him."

So when it was morning the old man took little
dog Turpie and was gone all day trying to sell him.

"You can have him for two shillings," said he to every person he met; but no one would buy him, and the old man had to bring little dog Turpie back home.

That night the Hobyahs came again and said,

"Hobyah! Hobyah! Hobyah! Tear down the hempstalks, eat up the old man and woman, and carry off the little girl!"

But little dog Turpie barked so that the Hobyahs all ran off; and the old man said, "Little dog

Turpie barks so that I cannot sleep nor slumber, and if I live till morning I will sell him!"

So when it was morning the old man took little dog Turpie and was gone all day trying to sell him. "You may have him for one shilling," said he to every person he met; but no one would buy him, and the old man had to bring little dog Turpie back home.

That night the
Hobyahs
came again
and said,
"Hobyah!
Hobyah! Hobyah! Tear down the hempstalks,
eat up the old man and woman, and carry off the
little girl!"

But little dog Turpie barked so that the Hobyahs
all ran off; and the old man said, "Little dog

Turpie barks so that I cannot sleep nor slumber,
and if I live till morning I will give little dog
Turpie away."

So when it was morning the old man took little
dog Turpie, and he was not gone long before he
gave little dog Turpie away, and he returned
without him.

That night
the Hobyahs
came again
and said,

"Hobyah! Hobyah! Hobyah! Tear down the hempstalks, eat up the old man and woman, and carry off the little girl!"

There was no little dog Turpie to bark this time, and the Hobyahs tore down the hempstalks, ate up the old man and woman, and carried the little girl off in a bag.

And when the Hobyahs came to where they  lived among the rocks in the forest they set the bag down with the little girl in it, and every Hobyah knocked on the top of the bag, and said, "Look me! look me!"

Then they crawled into the holes among the rocks and went to sleep, for the Hobyahs slept in the daytime.

The little girl cried a great deal, and a man with a big dog came that way and he heard her crying. So he opened the bag and asked her how she came there, and she told him. Then he put the dog in the bag and took the little girl to his home.

That night the Hobyahs went to the bag and knocked on the top of it and said, "Look me! look me!"

But when they opened the bag the big dog jumped out and ate them all up; so there are no Hobyahs now.

THE THREE BEARS

ONCE upon a time there was a little girl named Golden Hair, and she lived near a forest-covered mountain. Many pretty flowers grew in the woods on the mountain-side, and Golden Hair liked to gather them. Usually she did not go far from home after the flowers, but one day she rambled on and on, picking blossoms here and there, until she was much deeper in the woods than she had ever been before.

"Now I must go back," said Golden Hair at last. "I did n't intend to come such a long way and I 'm tired and hungry."

Just then she looked on ahead up the lonely hollow into which she had wandered, and there among the trees was as nice a little house as she had ever seen.

"I did n't know any one lived here in the woods," said Golden Hair. "I will go and find out whose house it is."

So she ran up to the door and rapped, but she got no response.

"Well," said she, "the people that belong to this house can't be far away, for I saw smoke coming out of the chimney. I suppose I might step in if the door isn't locked."

She lifted the latch, and the door was not locked, and she went in and looked about. The room in which she found herself was the kitchen, and a fire was burning in the fireplace, and on a table were three bowls of porridge — a big bowl, and a middle-sized bowl, and a little bowl.

"The people that live here have set the table for dinner, I think," said Golden Hair. "Oh, how hungry I am! I wonder if they would care if I ate some of their porridge without waiting till they came back. I will taste, anyway."

So she went to the table and took a spoonful of porridge from the big bowl.

"This is too hot," she said. "I will try the next."

Then she took a spoonful of porridge from the middle-sized bowl.

"This is not so hot as the other," said she, "but it is hotter than I like. I will try the next."

Then she took a spoonful of porridge from the little bowl, and that was just right and she ate it all.

"Now, I wish I could sit down to rest for a while

in a good easy chair," said Golden Hair. "They would have their easy chairs in the parlor, I suppose. I will look in and see."

So she went into the parlor and there she found three nice rocking-chairs, — a big chair, and a middle-sized chair, and a little chair. She tried the big chair, but it was too high.

"Dear me!" said Golden Hair, "I can't touch my feet to the floor. I don't like this chair, I will try the next." .

Then she tried the middle-sized chair. She could touch her feet to the floor in that, but it was too high for her to feel entirely comfortable, and she tried the little chair. That was just right, and she began rocking back and forth in it, when crack! smash! the chair broke and Golden Hair tumbled to the floor.

"That was a nice little chair," she said as she picked herself up. "I'm sorry it is broken. I was having such a good rest in it, too! I don't care for the other chairs, and I think I would like to lie down and have a nap. I must see where the beds are."

So she went upstairs and into a chamber, and there she found three beds — a big bed, and a middle-sized bed, and a little bed. She tried the

largest bed, and it was too hard. Then she tried
the middle-sized bed, and that was not so hard as
the big bed, but it was not soft enough to please
Golden Hair. Then she tried the little bed, and
that was just right, and she lay down on it and
covered herself up and fell fast asleep.

Now the house that Golden Hair was in belonged
to three bears — a big bear, a middle-sized bear, and
a little bear. Shortly before Golden Hair rapped
at their door they had cooked their porridge for
dinner and set it on the table. Then they had
gone out for a little walk to give the porridge time
to cool. While Golden Hair was asleep the bears
came home. As soon as they entered the kitchen
and looked at the table they saw that things were
not as they had left them.

"SOMEBODY HAS BEEN TASTING
MY PORRIDGE!" growled the big bear in his
great, gruff voice.

"AND SOMEBODY HAS BEEN TASTING MY POR-
RIDGE!" said the middle-sized bear.

"*And somebody has been tasting my porridge and
eaten it all up!*" piped the little bear.

"We will look around," said they, "and see if
there has been any more meddling."

Then they went into the parlor.

"SOMEBODY HAS BEEN SITTING IN MY CHAIR!" growled the big bear in his great, gruff voice.

"AND SOMEBODY HAS BEEN SITTING IN MY CHAIR!" said the middle-sized bear.

"*And somebody has been sitting in my chair and broken it all to pieces,*" piped the little bear.

Then they went upstairs to the chamber.

"SOMEBODY HAS BEEN TUMBLING MY BED!" growled the big bear in his great, gruff voice.

"AND SOMEBODY HAS BEEN TUMBLING MY BED!" said the middle-sized bear.

"*And somebody has been tumbling my bed, and here she is!*" piped the little bear.

Golden Hair waked up just then, and before the three bears could catch her she slipped from the bed and scrambled down the stairs and out at the door. Then she ran home as fast as her legs could carry her, and she never went near the three bears' house again.

TOM–TIT–TOT

ONCE upon a time there was a woman who baked five pies. But she left them in the oven too long, and when she took them out the crusts were so hard that she said to her daughter, "Put these pies on a shelf in the pantry and leave them there, and they'll come again."

She meant that the crusts would get soft presently, but that was not the way her daughter understood her; and the girl said to herself, "Well, if the pies will come again I'll eat them right now."

So she ate all the five pies. By and by it was supper-time, and the woman said, "Daughter, go you and get one of those pies. I dare say they've come again now."

The girl went into the pantry and looked, and there was nothing but the dishes. So back she came and said, "No, they're not come again."

"Not one of them?" asked the mother.

"Not one of them," replied the girl.

"Well," said the woman, "I'll have one for supper anyway."

"But you can't if none of them are come," said the girl.

"But I can," said the mother. "Go you and bring the best one."

"Best or worst," said the girl, "I've eaten them all, and I can't bring you one until one is come again."

Then the woman said no more, and after she had finished her supper she took her spinning to the door, and as she spun she sang,

"My daughter has eaten five, five pies to-day.
My daughter has eaten five, five pies to-day."

The king was coming down the street, and he heard her sing; but he did not catch the words. So he stopped and said, "What was that you were singing, my good woman?"

The woman was ashamed to let him know what her daughter had been doing, and in replying she changed her song to—

"My daughter has spun five, five skeins to-day.
My daughter has spun five, five skeins to-day."

"Stars of mine!" exclaimed the king, "I never

heard tell of any one who could do that. Such
talent is worth having."

Then he said, " Look you here, I want a wife
and I'll marry your daughter; and for eleven
months she shall have all she likes to eat, and all
the gowns she likes to get, and all the company
she likes to see. But the twelfth month she'll
have to spin five skeins every day or back I'll
send her to you."

" All right," said the woman, for she thought
what a grand marriage her daughter would be making; and as for the five skeins, the king would
very likely have forgotten all about them by the
end of eleven months.

So the king married the woman's daughter, and
the girl had all she liked to eat, and all the gowns
she liked to wear, and all the company she liked to
see. But when the eleven months were nearly over
she began to think about the skeins and to wonder
if the king had them in mind. Time went on,
and not one word did he say about the skeins until
the first day of the twelfth month. Then, early
in the morning, he took her into a room she
had never set eyes on before. There was nothing in it but a spinning-wheel and a stool and a
bed.

"Now, my dear," said the king, "I'll have some flax and some food sent you at once, and here you'll be shut in, and if you have n't spun five skeins by night, back you'll go to your mother."

Then the servants brought in flax and food enough to last for the day, and the king went off about his business. The queen was very much frightened, for she had never learned how to spin, and what was she to do with no one to come near her to help? She sat down and cried, but pretty soon she heard a soft rapping on the window. So she opened the window, and there on the ledge stood a queer little black man. He looked up at her and said, "What are you a-crying for?"

"Why do you ask?" said she.

"Never you mind," was his answer; "but tell me what you are a-crying for."

"It would do me no good if I did tell you," she said.

"You don't know that," said the little man.

"Well," said she, "it can do no harm, anyway;" and she told him all about the pies and the five skeins and everything.

"Then you think it's likely you won't be queen much longer, I suppose," said the little man when she finished. "But listen — this is what I'll do.

Every morning I'll come to your window and take the flax and bring it spun at night."

"And what do you expect me to pay you?" she asked.

The little black man looked out of the corners of his eyes and replied, "I will give you three guesses every night to guess my name, and if you have n't guessed it before the month is up, you shall be mine."

"I agree," said she; for she thought she would be sure to guess his name by the end of the month.

"Very well," said the little man, and he took the flax and went away.

The day passed and evening came. Then there was a knocking at the window, and when the window was opened the little black man stepped in with five skeins of flaxen thread on his arm. "Here it is," said he, "and now what's my name?"

"Is your name Bill?" said she.

"No, it is n't," said he.

"Is it Ned?" said she.

"No, it is n't," said he.

"Well, is it Joe?" said she.

"No, it is n't," said he, and then he laughed and winked and scurried out of the window.

When the king came in he found the five skeins ready for him. "I see I sha'n't have to send you back to your mother to-night," said he. "You have done very well, and I will have more food and flax brought to you in the morning."

So saying, he locked the door and went away. The days which followed were just like the first. Every morning a new supply of flax and food was left in the room, and the little black imp came regularly to get the flax and bring the skeins, and from sunrise to sunset the girl sat trying to think of names for him. But she could never seem to hit the right one. The end of the month got nearer and nearer, until the last day but one had come. The imp brought the five skeins at night as usual and said, " Well, have you guessed my name yet? "

" Is it Nicodemus? " said she.

" No, it is n't," said he.

" Is it Elijah? " said she.

" No, it is n't," said he.

" Is it Methuselah? " said she.

" No, it is n't," said he.

Then he looked at her with his eyes glowing like coals of fire, and he said, " Woman, there's only to-morrow night, and then you'll be mine; " and out he went through the window.

The little man had hardly gone when the queen heard the king coming along the passage. In he walked, and he glanced at the five skeins and said, "Well, my dear, it seems to be pretty certain now that I sha'n't have to send you back to your mother, and I'm going to eat my supper in here with you to-night."

Pretty soon the servants brought in dishes and food and another stool, and the two sat down and ate. But the king had only taken three or four mouthfuls when he stopped and began to laugh.

"What is there to laugh about?" asked the queen.

"Why," said he, "I was out hunting to-day, and as I was climbing a high hill among the forest trees I heard a sort of humming sound. So I got off my horse and I went along very softly and soon I came in sight of a little hut, and before the hut burned a fire, and beside the fire sat the funniest little black imp that ever was; and he had a tiny spinning wheel on which he was spinning like mad; and as he spun he sang,

> 'Nimmy, nimmy not,
> My name's Tom-Tit-Tot.'"

When the girl heard the king repeat these words she wanted to jump up and clap her hands, but she never stirred or said a word.

The next day the little man got the flax at the accustomed time, and in the evening he was back with it nicely spun in five handsome skeins. He

knocked at the window-panes, and when the queen let him in he was grinning from ear to ear. "What's my name?" he said as he gave her the skeins.

"Is it Spindleshanks?" said she.

"No, it is n't," said he.

"Is it Cowribs?" said she.

"No, it is n't," said he, and he laughed loud and long. "Take time, woman," he advised. "Next guess and you are mine, ha! ha! ha!" and he stretched out his black arms toward her.

But the queen pointed her finger at him and said,

> "Nimmy, nimmy not,
> Your name's Tom-Tit-Tot."

At that the little black man gave an awful shriek. "Some witch told you! Some witch told you!" he cried. Then he dashed out of the window into the dark and she never saw him any more.

THE KING OF THE GOLDEN
MOUNTAIN

ACERTAIN merchant sent two richly laden
ships on a voyage. He invested all his
property in them, and he hoped to make
great gains; but the ships were wrecked, and the
merchant was reduced from wealth to poverty and
had to live in a poor little cottage.

One day, as he was walking along by the sea-
shore thinking sadly of his future, a rough-looking
dwarf stood before him and asked why he was so
sorrowful.

"I would tell you," said the merchant, "if it
would do any good."

"Who knows but that it may?" said the little
man. "Tell me your troubles and perhaps I can
be of some service."

Then the merchant related how all his wealth
had gone to the bottom of the sea.

"Oh, well, don't mourn any longer about that,"
said the dwarf. "Only promise that twelve years

hence you will bring to me here whatever meets you first on your return home, and I will see that you shall never want for gold."

The merchant promised and thought he had the best of the bargain; but when he approached his home, who should come running to meet him but his little boy. The merchant was greatly distressed to think that he had bound himself to give his boy to the dwarf. "Very likely, though, the dwarf was only joking," said he; "for I see no sign of that gold he told me I was to have."

A few days afterward the merchant was cleaning out an old lumber-room, and under a heap of rubbish in a corner he found a box full of gold pieces. Then he was fearful that the dwarf was in earnest. However, there was the gold, and what was he to do with it? He concluded to go into business once more, and he was not long in becoming richer than he had been before.

Time went on, and the son grew up and the end of the twelve years drew near. The merchant was very anxious now, and one day he told his son about his promise to the dwarf.

"Well," said the son, "I would not worry; perhaps things may not turn out as badly as you think."

The merchant begs the dwarf not to take his son from him

When the appointed date came they went together to the sea-shore, and there they found the little dwarf. The merchant begged the dwarf not to insist on taking his son from him, and they argued for a long time. At last the dwarf said, "I will yield up my rights on one condition, which is that your son shall get into an open boat and be set adrift on the sea without sail or oars."

"Oh, cruel dwarf!" said the merchant. "If I must choose between the sea and you I choose the sea."

Then the dwarf led the way to a boat that was drawn up on the beach near where they had been talking. They dragged the boat to the water, the son got in, and the dwarf pushed it off.

The merchant hoped his son would drift to shore, but the wind and currents carried the little boat farther and farther away until he could see it no longer. Then he hoped his son would be rescued by some vessel, but the weeks and months slipped away without his hearing anything from him, and finally he gave his son up for lost.

However, the young man was not drowned in the sea as his father thought. He sat securely in the little boat, and it rocked along over the waves until it was wafted to the shores of a country the merchant's son had never before seen. Not far from where he came to land was a lofty mountain, and the color of the mountain was yellow, like gold, and on its summit was a beautiful castle.

So the merchant's son walked away from the sea and climbed the golden mountain; but when he reached the castle he discovered that it was empty and desolate, for it was enchanted. He went all through the great building and saw not a living thing till he entered one of the chambers where he found a white snake; and this white snake spoke to him.

"Oh, how glad I am to see you!" it said. "I am not really a snake. A wicked dwarf has enchanted me. I am the Queen of the Golden Mountain. Twelve long years have I waited for a deliverer."

"If you will tell me in what way I can be of service to you," said the merchant's son, "I will do anything I can to disenchant you."

"Then listen to me," said the queen. "This night twelve black men will come and they will ask you why you are here; but be silent. Give them no answer. Let them do what they will, even if they beat and torment you. Speak not a word, or you cannot save me. At twelve o'clock they will go. The second night twelve other black men will come, and they will do as did the first twelve. The third night twelve more black men will come and they will try their worst to make you speak; but if you withstand them till the twelfth hour of that night I shall be free."

"Have no fear," replied the young man; "your wishes shall be obeyed."

Everything came to pass as the queen had said, and the merchant's son was threatened and beaten and tormented. Yet he spoke not a word, and at twelve o'clock on the third night the black men hastened away howling with rage and disappointment. Then the white snake became a beautiful young queen. The castle, too, was disenchanted and was all that the home of a queen should be; and the merchant's son fell in love with the queen, and she fell in love with him. So it was not long before a wedding was celebrated in the castle, and the merchant's son became the King of the Golden Mountain.

Eight years passed, and then the king said, "I must go to visit my father. In all the years I have been here he has had no word from me, and he must think I am dead."

"No, no," said the queen, "do not go."

But the king grew more and more anxious to return to his father, and at last the queen consented. When he was about to start she gave him a wishing-ring, and said, " Take this ring and put it on your finger. You have but to turn it around when you wish and whatever you wish for will be granted. Only promise that you will not make use of it to bring me hence to your father's."

He promised what she asked and put the ring on his finger. Then he wished himself near the town where his father lived. A moment later he found himself at the town gates; but the clothes he wore were so different from those worn by the people of that region that the town guards were suspicious and would not let him in. So he walked off across the fields trying to think what he would do next.

Presently he came to a shepherd's hut. " I will make an exchange of clothes here," said he, and he sought out the shepherd and offered him a golden guinea for some of his old garments.

The shepherd was very glad to part with them at that price, and when the king put them on and left his own fine apparel behind, the shepherd could only think that the poor man had lost his wits.

The king now went back to the town, and, in his shepherd's garb, the guards supposed him to be a peasant and let him pass without question. He hastened to his father's house, and told the merchant that he was his son.

" But my son is dead, long since," said the merchant; and he would not believe it possible that this ragged fellow was his son, whom he had seen disappear eight years previous in the little boat.

" Is there no mark by which you would know if I am really your son? " the king asked at length.

" Yes," replied the merchant, " my son had a mark like a raspberry on the under side of his right arm, just above the elbow."

Then the king pulled up the sleeve on his right arm and showed the mark, and the merchant was satisfied that the young man was his son, and he listened with wonder while the son related how he had married a queen and was King of the Golden Mountain.

" What! " cried the merchant, "you tell me you are a king? That cannot be true, else you would not be travelling about in a shepherd's frock."

The son was very much troubled when his father did not believe him. " I will prove to you that I speak the truth," said he, and forgetting his promise to his queen he turned his ring and wished to have her there with him.

Instantly she stood before him in her royal robes, and the merchant could not doubt longer that his son was King of the Golden Mountain as he had said. But the queen wept because the king had broken his word. She stopped crying presently, yet she did not forget his broken promise, and that night while he was asleep she drew the ring from his finger and wished herself at home in her kingdom. When the king awoke he was alone, and the ring was gone from his finger. He was very sorrowful then, and he said, " I will journey forth into the world and perhaps I can find my kingdom again."

So saying, he set out and travelled for many days. At last he came near to a hill on the top of which he heard loud and angry voices. " I must find out what is going on here," said the king, and he climbed the hill and crept along till he was near enough to see that two giants were disputing over the possession of a cloak and a pair of boots.

He listened and learned that the cloak made its wearer invisible, and that the boots carried the person who put them on wherever he wished to

go.   The giants began a desperate struggle, when
one of them said, " Why should we kill each other?

Let us bury the things that make the trouble
between us right here and have no more to do
with them."

"Yes," said the other, "let us bury them."

So they scraped a hole in the dirt, threw in the
cloak and boots, covered them up and went off.

Then the king ran to the spot where the cloak and boots were buried and dug them up, and when he had shaken the dirt out of them he put them on. They fitted perfectly, for they were magic garments that increased or decreased in size to suit the stature of the wearer. " Now," said he, " I wish I was back at the Golden Mountain."

He was there at once; but no one knew he had come because the cloak he had on made him invisible. He found the queen very melancholy on account of her long separation from him. " I would wish him back," said she, looking at the ring on her finger, "if he had not broken his promise."

This she said again and again, and at length the tears gathered in her eyes and she said, " I cannot bear to have him away any longer," and she turned the ring and said, " I wish he was here."

But the king was already there, only she could not see him. She looked about disappointed. " Can it be that the magic is gone from my ring?" she exclaimed. " I will try again."

She turned the ring once more and this time she said, " I wish to be carried to the king."

As the king was in the same room there was nothing for the ring to do, and she remained just where she was. Then the king took pity on her and threw off the cloak he was wearing, and the queen saw him and they ran to each other's arms. The king was happy and the queen was happy, and they lived happily together on the Golden Mountain ever after.

LITTLE RED RIDING-HOOD

ONCE upon a time there was a little girl who lived in a village near a forest, and she was such a nice little girl that every one was very fond of her. When she went anywhere she always wore a little red riding-hood her grandmother had given her, and so people called her " Little Red Riding-Hood."

One day her mother, who had just made some custards, said to her, " My dear, you shall go and see how your grandmother is ; and you may take her a custard and a little cake of butter. I will put them in a basket that you can carry on your arm."

Little Red Riding-Hood was soon on the way to her grandmother's cottage, which was in the forest, a half hour's walk from the village. But she had not gone far into the woods when she met a wolf.

" Good day, little girl," said the wolf.

He was very polite, though at the same time he was wishing he could eat her; and that is what he would have done had he not been afraid of some wood-cutters who were at work near by.

"Where are you going, my pretty little lady?" he asked.

"I am going to see my grandmother," she replied, "and I am taking her a custard and a cake of butter from my mother."

"And where does she live?" the wolf inquired.

"Oh," said Little Red Riding-Hood, "you keep right along this road, and she lives in the first house."

"Well, good by," said the wolf. "I'm going to be passing your grandmother's and I will stop and tell her you are coming to see her."

Then the wolf ran on, and when he arrived at the grandmother's house he went to the door and knocked — tap, tap!

He got no answer, and he knocked louder — slam, slam!

But still there was no response, and after a minute he stood on his hind legs and reached up one of his forepaws to the latch and opened the door. He found not a soul in the house; for the grandmother had gone to market in the town. She had started early and had left her bed unmade and her nightcap lying on the pillow.

"I know what I'll do," said the wolf; and after shutting the door he put the grandmother's night-

cap on his head and lay down in the bed and drew
the covers up over himself.

Meanwhile Little Red Riding-Hood was coming
along the forest road. She did not hurry. Sometimes she stopped to pick flowers, and sometimes
she paused to hear the birds singing among the
trees. But presently she reached her grandmother's
cottage and knocked at the door — tap, tap !

"Who is there?" asked the wolf, softening his
rough voice as much as he could.

"It's me, Granny — your Little Red Riding-
Hood," she replied; and then she said, "Are you
sick, Granny? Your voice is very hoarse."

"I have a cold," answered the wolf, "and I am
not feeling well enough to get up to-day. You can
press your finger on the latch and come in."

So Little Red Riding-Hood pressed her finger
on the latch and opened the door and went in.
"I have brought you a custard, dear Granny," said
she, "and a cake of butter from my mama, and
some flowers that I picked in the forest."

"You can put your basket on the table and take
off your hood," said the wolf.

Little Red Riding-Hood put the basket on
the table, and after she had taken off her hood
she went to the bedside. "Oh, Grandmama,

Grandmama," said she, "what hairy arms you have ! "

" All the better to hug you with, my dear," the wolf replied.

" And oh, Grandmama, what great ears you have!" said little Red Riding-Hood.

" All the better to hear you with, my dear," the wolf replied.

" And oh, Grandmama, what great eyes you have ! " said Little Red Riding-Hood.

" All the better to see you with, my dear," the wolf replied.

" And oh, Grandmama, what a long nose you have ! " said Little Red Riding-Hood.

" All the better to smell the sweet flowers you have brought me," the wolf replied.

" And oh, Grandmama, what great white teeth you have ! " said Little Red Riding-Hood.

" All the better to gobble you up with ! " cried the wicked wolf, and he leaped from the bed toward Little Red Riding-Hood with his mouth wide open.

But while the wolf and the little girl had been talking the grandmother had come home from market. She looked in at the door and saw the wolf in her bed, and then she ran to the woodpile in the yard and got an ax. Just as the wolf sprang toward Little Red Riding-Hood the grandmother rushed in at the door with the ax and gave the wolf such a blow that it killed him, and Little Red Riding-Hood was not harmed at all.

THE FOUR MUSICIANS

THERE was once a donkey who had worked for his master faithfully many years, but his strength at last began to fail, and every day he became more and more unfit for work. Finally his master concluded it was no longer worth while to keep him and was thinking of putting an end to him. But the donkey saw that mischief was brewing and he ran away. "I will go to the city," said he, "and like enough I can get an engagement there as a musician; for though my body has grown weak, my voice is as strong as ever."

So the donkey hobbled along toward the city, but he had not gone far when he spied a dog lying by the roadside and panting as if he had run a long way. "What makes you pant so, my friend?" asked the donkey.

"Alas!" replied the dog, "my master was going to knock me on the head because I am old and weak and can no longer make myself useful to him in hunting. So I ran away; but how am I to gain a living now, I wonder?"

"Hark ye!" said the donkey. "I am going to the city to be a musician. You may as well keep company with me and try what you can do in the same line."

The dog said he was willing, and they went on together. Pretty soon they came to a cat sitting in the middle of the road and looking as dismal as three wet days. "Pray, my good lady," said the donkey, "what is the matter with you, for you seem quite out of spirits?"

"Ah me!" responded the cat, "how can I be cheerful when my life is in danger? I am getting old, my teeth are blunt, and I like sitting by the fire and purring better than chasing the mice about. So this morning my mistress laid hold of me and was going to drown me. I was lucky enough to get away from her; but I do not know what is to become of me, and I'm likely to starve."

"Come with us to the city," said the donkey, "and be a musician. You understand serenading, and with your talent for that you ought to be able to make a very good living."

The cat was pleased with the idea and went along with the donkey and the dog. Soon after-

ward, as they were passing a farmyard, a rooster
flew up on the gate and screamed out with all his
might, " Cock-a-doodle-doo ! "

" Bravo ! " said the donkey, " upon my word you
make a famous noise ; what is it all about ? "

" Oh," replied the rooster, " I was only foretelling
fine weather for our washing-day ; and that I do
every week. But would you believe it ! My
mistress does n't thank me for my pains, and she
has told the cook that I must be made into broth
for the guests that are coming next Sunday."

"Heaven forbid!" exclaimed the donkey; "come.
with us, Master Chanticleer. It will be better, at
any rate, than staying here to have your head cut
off. We are going to the city to be musicians ;
and — who knows? — perhaps the four of us can get
up some kind of a concert. You have a good voice,
and if we all make music together, it will be something striking. So come along."

"With all my heart," said the cock ; and the
four ·went on together.

The city was, however, too far away for them to
reach it on the first day of their travelling, and
when, toward night, they came to a thick woods,
they decided to turn aside from the highway and
pass the night among the trees. So they found a

dry, sheltered spot at the foot of a great oak and the donkey and dog lay down on the ground beneath it; but the cat climbed up among the branches, and the rooster, thinking the higher he sat the safer he would be, flew up to the very top.   Before he went to sleep the rooster looked around him to the four points of the compass to make sure that everything was all right.   In so doing he saw in the distance a little light shining, and he called out to his companions, " There must be a house no great way off, for I can see a light."

" If that be the case," said the donkey, " let us get up and go there.   Our lodging here is not what I am used to, and the sooner we change it for better the more pleased I shall be."

" Yes," said the dog, " and perhaps I might be able to get a few bones with a little meat on them at that house."

" And very likely I might get some milk," said the cat.

" And there ought to be some scraps of food for me," said the rooster.

So the cat and the rooster came down out of the tree and they all walked off with Chanticleer in the lead toward the spot where he had seen the light. At length they drew near the house, and the donkey,

being the tallest of the company, went up to the
lighted window and looked in.

"Well, what do you see?" asked the dog.

"What do I
see?" answered
the donkey. "I
see that this is a
robber's house.
There are swords
and pistols and
blunderbusses on
the walls, and there
are chests of money
on the floor,
and all sorts
of other plunder
lying about. The
robbers are
sitting at a
table that is
loaded with
the best
of eat-
ables and
drinkables,
and they

and flew into his face, spitting and scratching. Then
he cried out in fright and ran toward the door, and
the dog, who was lying there, bit the robber's leg.
He managed, however, to get out in the yard, and
there the donkey struck out with a hind foot and
gave him a kick that knocked him down, and
Chanticleer who had been roused by the noise, cried
out "Cock-a-doodle-doo ! Cock-a-doodle-doo ! "

The robber captain had barely strength to crawl
away to the other robbers. "We cannot live at
that house any more," said he. " In the kitchen is
a grewsome witch, and I felt her hot breath and her
long nails on my face, and by the door there stood
a man who stabbed me in the leg, and in the yard
is a black giant who beat me with a club, and on the
roof is a little fellow who kept shouting, 'Chuck
him up to me ! Chuck him up to me ! ' "

So the robbers went away and never came back,
and the four musicians found themselves so well
pleased with their new quarters that they did not
go to the city, but stayed where they were ; and I
dare say you would find them there at this very
day.

TEENY-TINY

ONCE upon a time there was a teeny-tiny woman lived in a teeny-tiny house in a teeny-tiny village. One day this teeny-tiny woman put on her teeny-tiny bonnet and went out of her teeny-tiny house to take a teeny-tiny walk. And when the teeny-tiny woman had gone a teeny-tiny way she came to a teeny-tiny gate; and the teeny-tiny woman opened the teeny-tiny gate and went into a teeny-tiny field. And when the teeny-tiny woman had gone into the teeny-tiny field she saw a teeny-tiny bone beside a teeny-tiny tree, and the teeny-tiny woman said to her teeny-tiny self, "This teeny-tiny bone will make me some teeny-tiny soup for my teeny-tiny supper."

So the teeny-tiny woman put the teeny-tiny bone into her teeny-tiny pocket and went home to her teeny-tiny house. And when the teeny-tiny woman got home to her teeny-tiny house she was a teeny-tiny tired, and she went up her teeny-tiny stairs to her teeny-tiny chamber and put the teeny-tiny bone into a teeny-tiny cupboard. Then she went to sleep in her teeny-tiny bed, and when she had been asleep a teeny-tiny time she was awakened by a

teeny-tiny voice from the teeny-tiny cupboard which said : —

"Give me my bone!"

And the teeny-tiny woman was a teen-tiny frightened. So she hid her teeny-tiny head under the teeny-tiny clothes and went to sleep again.

And when she had been asleep for a teeny-tiny time, the teeny-tiny voice cried out again from the teeny-tiny cupboard a teeny-tiny louder : —

"Give me my bone!"

This made the teeny-tiny woman a teeny-tiny more frightened. So she hid her teeny-tiny head a teeny-tiny farther under the teeny-tiny clothes. And when the teeny-tiny woman had been asleep again a teeny-tiny time, the teeny-tiny voice from the teeny-tiny cupboard said again a teeny-tiny louder : —

"Give me my bone!"

And the teeny-tiny woman was a teeny-tiny more frightened ; but she put her teeny-tiny head out of the teeny-tiny clothes and said in her loudest teeny-tiny voice : —

"TAKE IT!"

THE WOLF AND THE SEVEN
LITTLE GOSLINGS

ONCE there was a goose who had seven little goslings of whom she was very fond, and she did everything she could for them. What troubled her most was to keep them safe from a big gray wolf who lived near by in the forest, and who sometimes came prowling around the house that the goose lived in. Whenever she had to go out to look for food she called the goslings all together and said, " Dear children, I am obliged to leave you for a little while to go and get something for us to eat. Take care of yourselves and do not let the wolf come in. You will know him by his rough voice and his black paws. If he once gets in the house he will eat you."

The goslings always replied, " Oh, we will be very careful, dear mother. You need not worry about us."

One day, when the mother goose had gone out to get food, the wolf came to the house and rapped, and said in his rough voice, " Dear children, open the door. I am your mother. I have brought you something very nice."

The seven little goslings made answer, "You are not our mother. She has a fine, sweet voice. Your voice is rough. You are the wolf, and we will not open the door."

Then the wolf bethought himself of a trick. He went to a shopkeeper and said, " Give me a great piece of chalk."

The shopkeeper gave the wolf the chalk, and the wolf ate it, and it made his voice fine and sweet. Then he went back to the house of the seven little goslings and said with his fine, sweet voice, " Dear children, let me come in. I am your mother, and every one of you shall have something to eat."

But the seven little goslings looked through the crack beneath the door and saw his black paws. Then they said, "Oho! our mother does not have black feet. You are the wolf, and we will not open the door."

So the wolf went to a baker and said, " Baker, sprinkle my feet with flour."

The baker did not wish to do this, but the wolf said, " If you do not obey I will eat you."

So the baker strewed the wolf's feet with flour, and the wolf went back to the seven little goslings and said, "Dear children, open the door. I am your mother, and every one of you shall have something to eat."

The wolf's voice was sweet and fine, and when the little goslings looked under the door and saw the wolf's paws as white as snow, they thought he was their mother. They opened the door and the wolf leaped in.

The goslings were very much frightened then and they hid themselves as quickly as they could. One went under the table, the second into the bed, the third into the oven, the fourth behind the meal-chest, the fifth in a closet, the sixth beneath a great pot, and the seventh went into the clock. But the wolf found them all and ate them except the youngest, who was in the clock, and then he went away.

Shortly afterward the mother goose came home. The door was open! Tables and chairs were overturned! the kitchen pots were broken! the bedclothes were on the floor! and, what was worse, the children were gone! Nowhere could she find them. Then she called them each by name, and there was nothing but silence in response until she came to the name of the youngest, when a little squeaking voice answered, " Dear mother, I am in the clock."

She pulled him out, and he related to her what had happened.

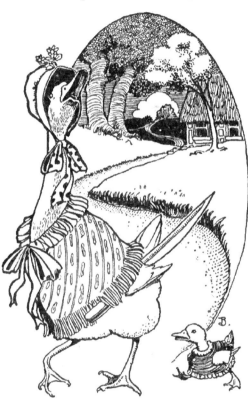

The old goose said to the little one, " Come with me. I will take the carving knife, and we will see if we can find that wicked wolf. He has not gone far. After eating so much he has lain down somewhere to sleep."

So the mother goose took the carving knife and set forth with the little gosling close behind her. They followed the wolf's tracks into a meadow, and there they found him fast asleep and snoring.

" Here he is," whispered the mother goose.

" No doubt he feels very comfortable after eating six of my children for his supper."

Then she stole up to the wolf and gave him a blow with the carving knife that killed him. After that she cut him open and out stepped the six little goslings one by one ; for he had swallowed them whole and they were more frightened than hurt. They were very glad to escape from their dark prison, and as they walked along behind the mother goose toward home, there never were happier goslings in the world than they were.

THE MAGIC FIDDLE

A FARMER once had a servant who worked for him three years without being paid any wages. The servant did his work well and faithfully, and was the first of the farmer's help to get up in the morning and the last to go to bed at night. If there was any hard work to be done which no one else would do he was always ready to undertake it. He never made any complaint, and never failed to be good-natured and contented. But at last it came into the man's head that he would not continue without pay any longer. So he went to his master and said, "I have worked hard for you a long time, and now I think I should have some money for my labor."

The farmer was miserly and not altogether honest, and as he knew that his man was very simple-hearted he took out his purse and gave him three-pence. "There is a penny," said he, "for each year you have served me."

The servant thought threepence was a great deal of money to have, and he said to himself, "Why should I work here any longer? I can now travel into the wide world and make myself merry."

Then, with his money jingling in his pocket, he set out roaming over hill and valley. As he tramped singing along the road a little dwarf hopped out of a wayside bush and asked, "What makes you so happy, sir?"

"Why! what should make me downhearted?" said the man. "I am sound in health and rich in purse. I have saved up the pay for three years' work and have it all safe in my pocket."

"How much may that come to?" inquired the dwarf.

"Full threepence," replied the servant.

"Listen," said the dwarf. "I wish you would give the threepence to me. I am very poor."

When the man heard this he was so sorry for the dwarf that he gave him the threepence; and the little dwarf said, "As you have been so kind to me I will grant any wish that you may care to make; so choose whatever you like."

"Aha!" said the servant. "You are a wonder-worker, I see," and, greatly rejoiced at his good luck, he paused to think what he most wanted. "I like many things better than money," said he. "Now if you could give me a fiddle that would set every one dancing who hears me play on it, that would please me more than anything else I can think of."

"All right," said the dwarf, "you can have what you ask for;" and out of a bag he carried he pulled a fiddle and bow and handed them to his companion.

"Heart alive! what more can one desire?" said the servant.

Then the dwarf went his way and the hired man walked on singing as before. But he had not gone far when an old man called to him from a roadside field. The old man had an ax in his hands and was standing under a great oak-tree that he had begun to cut down. "This work is too hard for me," said the old man. "But a stout fellow like you would make nothing of it, and if you will finish chopping through this tree-trunk I will pay you five shillings."

"Give me the ax," said the servant. "I am quite willing to earn a little money, for mine is all gone;" and he threw off his coat and went to work.

By and by the oak crashed to the ground. "There," said the servant, "now I'll take my five shillings and be stepping along."

"I did not think you could do the work so soon or I would not have offered you so much," said the old man.

"Well, that is no fault of mine," the servant replied.

"But five shillings is more than the work is worth," argued the old man. "Here, I will give you three shillings, and that is a great plenty."

"No, I will take nothing less than what you agreed to give me in the first place," the servant declared.

"Then you will not get anything," said the other.

"We will see about that," was the servant's response, and he took up his fiddle and began playing, and the old man began to dance.

"How is this?" the old man cried. "Is that fiddle enchanted?"

"Yes," said the servant.

"Then for heaven's sake, my good fellow, play no more!" shouted the old man. "I don't want to dance. My bones are too stiff for me to be springing about like this. Master, master! do let the fiddle alone."

"You don't like dancing, eh?" laughed the servant. "Well, it is good enough for you after treating me so meanly;" and he played away more briskly than ever.

"Have pity, have pity!" begged the old man, "and I will give you your money."

So the servant stopped fiddling. Then the old man handed over the five shillings; but he was so angry that as soon as he had rubbed his aching joints he hurried to the town, muttering as he went, "The miserable fiddler! Just wait — I will get even with him."

As soon as he reached the town he complained to the constables that he had been robbed. "You will know the rascal who robbed me easily enough," said the old man; "for he is always singing, and he carries a violin under his arm."

The constables set off at once in search of the rogue, and presently they caught him and brought him before the court to be tried.

"That is he," said the old man, "that is the very fellow who stole my five shillings."

"No," said the servant. "I did not steal. You gave me the money for playing a tune to you on my fiddle."

"What!" exclaimed the judge, "five shillings for

" Have pity, have pity !" begged the old man

a tune on a fiddle! That's not at all likely. I fear you are a liar as well as a thief."

"I speak the truth," said the servant.

"Heaven defend us!" screamed the old man. "His lies are as thick as flies on the wall. He stole my money, and you can't believe a word he says."

"Prisoner," said the judge, "you deserve hanging."

Then the judge turned to the officers and said, "Take the five shillings from him and give them to the old man; and after that you may conduct the culprit to the gallows."

So the officers took away the servant's money and marched him off to the gallows, while the old man cried after him, "You vagabond! You dog of a fiddler! Now you will get your just deserts."

A crowd followed the culprit to the place of execution, and the officers were about to put the rope around his neck when he said to the judge, "My lord, grant me one last request."

"What is it?" asked the judge.

"Only this," replied the servant — "that I may play on my fiddle once more."

"Very well," replied the judge, "play away."

"Oh, no, no!" shouted the old man, "for mercy's sake don't let him play his fiddle."

But the judge said, " It is only for this once ; he will soon have done."

" Then bind me fast, oh, bind me fast before he begins," cried the old man.

The servant wasted no time in starting a tune, and at the first scrape all the people began to wag their heads — his accuser and the judge, the officers, the jailer, the hangman, and every one else who was within hearing.   They could not help themselves.

At the second scrape they all lifted their legs and the hangman let go his hold of the honest servant to make ready to dance.

At the third scrape they one and all leaped into the air, and began to caper about — old and young, fat and lean, danced as hard as they could.   Even the dogs got up on their hind legs and pranced about with the rest.   The dancing was merry and pleasant enough at first, but when it had gone on for a while and there seemed to be no end to the playing or leaping, the people began to cry out for the servant to stop fiddling.   But that he would not do till the judge had promised he should not be hanged, and the old man had given back to him his five shillings.

So the judge promised and the old man handed over the money.   Then the servant tucked the fiddle under his arm and started off again on his travels, and the people who had been dancing around the gallows heard him singing as he walked down the street out of the town.

THE CLEVER WIFE

ONCE there was a famous castle-builder by the name of Gobborn Seer, and he had a son called Jack. In the course of time Jack grew to be a young man, and the old castle-builder began to think of teaching him his trade and leaving his business to him. "Jack is a good boy," said he ; "but he is not quick with his brains. I must see what I can do for his education."

So one day he sent Jack to sell a sheepskin, and he said to him, "You must bring me back the skin and the value of it as well."

Jack went, but he could not find any one who would leave him the skin and give him its price, too, and he came home discouraged.

"Never mind," said his father, "you can try again to-morrow."

The next day Jack went out once more with the skin, but nobody wished to buy it on such terms.

"Well," said his father, when Jack returned home, "so you have not sold the skin yet ? However, go out to-morrow and your luck may be better."

On the third day Jack set off as before and
trudged hither and yon till nearly nightfall and
could not find a customer who would pay him for
the skin without having it. At last he came to
a bridge across a little river, and when he was half
way over the bridge he stopped and leaned on the
parapet, thinking of his troubles. " I shall never
be able to get rid of this horrid sheepskin if I live
to be as old as Methuselah," said he. " I 'm thinking I 'd better run away from home and have quit
of the job."

While he was talking to himself thus he looked
over the side of the bridge and saw a girl washing
clothes on the border of the stream. At the same
time she looked up and saw him, and said, " If it
may be no offence asking, what is it you feel so
badly about?"

Jack held up the sheepskin that she might see it,
and replied, " My father has given me this skin
to sell, and I am to fetch it back and the price of
it besides."

" Is that all?" laughed the girl. " Such a task
ought not to trouble you in the least. Bring the
skin down here."

Jack carried it down to her and she washed it
in the stream and took the wool from it. Then

she paid him its value and kept the wool, but gave him the skin to carry back.

When Jack reached home he told his father all that had happened, and his father said, "That was a clever woman you met at the bridge, and she would make you a good wife. Do you think you could find her again?"

"I think so," replied Jack.

"Well, then," his father said, "you go and see if she is at the same place to-morrow, and if she is there, bid her come home with you and take a cup of tea with us."

The young fellow did as his father suggested, and, sure enough, he found the girl at the waterside and told her how his old father had a wish to meet her, and would she be pleased to take tea with them?

The girl thanked him kindly and accepted the invitation. When she came the old man did not have to talk with her long to assure himself that she was uncommonly keen-witted, and then he asked her if she would marry his Jack.

"Yes," said she, and they were married.

Not long afterward Gobborn Seer told his son he must come with him and build the finest castle that ever was seen. The castle was to be for their

king, who wished to outdo all the other kings in
the world with his wonderful castle. So they set
off for the place where the castle was to stand, and,
as they walked along, the old man said to Jack,
"Can you not shorten the way for me?"

"It is many long miles we have to go," replied
Jack, "and I would shorten them if I could, but
I fear that is not possible."

"Ah, well!" said the old man, "if you cannot
shorten the way, you are no good to me and had
better go back home."

So poor Jack returned, and when he entered the
house door his wife cried out, "Why! how is it
that you are back so soon?"

He told her what his father had said and what
he had replied.

"You stupid!" said his clever wife, "why did n't
you tell a tale? That would have shortened the
road! He would have forgotten the miles and
the weariness. Now listen till I repeat to you a
story, and then you catch up with your father and
begin it at once. He will like hearing it, and by
the time it is done you will have arrived where the
castle is to be."

Jack heard the story, and then he ran as fast as
he could until he overtook his father. The old

man said never a word, but Jack began his story, and the road was shortened as his wife had said.

At the end of their journey they found many workmen assembled and waiting for them. The workmen had been sent there by the king to labor under the direction of the old castle-builder and his son, and without delay they were set to laying the foundations of the castle. For a year the builders worked, and Gobborn Seer and Jack and their helpers had erected such a castle that thousands came to admire it. Last of all the king came also. " Is the castle done? " he asked.

" I have just a ceiling to finish in an upper hall," replied Gobborn Seer, " and then it will want nothing."

" Very well," said the king, " I shall return to-morrow and pay you for your labor."

But after the king had gone a friendly courtier sent for Gobborn and his son and told them he had learned that the king was so afraid they would now build some other king as fine a castle as his that he meant on the morrow to throw them into prison and keep them there for the rest of their lives.

" That sounds bad," said the old man to Jack, " but keep a good heart and we will come off all right yet."

The next day, when the king arrived, Gobborn told him he had been unable to complete the upper hall for lack of a certain tool. "I shall have to go home for that tool," said he.

"No, no!" exclaimed the king, "you can send just as well."

"Yes, I might send Jack, I suppose," the old man responded.

"Don't do that," the king said; "it will be better to have Jack here with you. Let one of the workmen do the errand."

"But the tool I want is a very delicate one," explained Gobborn, "and there's not a workman among them all to whom I would trust it."

"Well, then, what would you say to having my own son do the errand for you?" asked the king.

"Let him go, by all means," Gobborn replied, "and I will send a note by him to Jack's wife telling her where to find the tool."

Then he wrote this message: "I need my seequir. It is in the big tool chest in the attic. Don't let the prince who does this errand return without it."

"Jack," said the old castle-builder when the prince had gone, "if your wife is as clever as I think she is we can rest easy now. That message will give her a hint of what she is to do, and we can trust her to accomplish the rest."

As soon as Jack's wife read the letter the prince brought she saw that something was wrong. "There is no such tool as a seequir," she thought, "and that big chest in the attic is empty; and yet the note says for me not to let the prince return without the tool. Well, I won't."

Then she said to the prince, "I think I shall have to ask you to help me get that tool."

"I am at your service, madam," replied the prince with a polite bow.

So Jack's wife led the way to the attic and said, "Here is the big chest. I will lift the lid and you must reach down into the bottom of the chest after the tool."

"With pleasure," responded the prince, but no sooner had he leaned over with his head and arms in the chest than Jack's wife gave him a shove that tumbled him into the big box, heels and all, and then she slammed down the cover and locked it. Next she hunted up an augur and bored some holes in the lid to let in a little air and light to the prisoner.

"Now, Prince," said she, "I want to know what is the matter with my husband and his father."

The prince did not wish to say.

"You are going to tell me the whole story," ordered Jack's wife, "and if you don't start with it right off I shall bring up a kettle of hot water

from the fire and pour some through these augur holes. That will loosen your tongue, I'll be bound."

So the prince told how Gobborn Seer and his son were going to be imprisoned.

"We'll have to put a stop to such doings," said Jack's wife. "Do you hear me, Prince? — you and I will have to put a stop to such doings."

"Yes," replied the prince, "I hear you."

He did not feel much like arguing, shut up in that box with those augur holes in the lid that only

let in a little light and air, but which might admit
a good deal of hot water.

"Very well," said Jack's wife, "I'm going to
get some paper and a pen and ink, and I'll slip
them in through these holes to you. Then you
can write a letter to the king, your father, and let
him know that you will never return alive unless
the old castle-builder and his son are released."

She got the writing materials and poked them
through the augur holes to the prince, and he wrote
as she directed.

The letter frightened the king and he at once
paid Gobborn for his work and let him and his
son go to their home.

"Jack," said his father, as they were on the way,
"your wife has helped us nobly. You ought now
to reward her by building a castle for her far finer
than the one we have made for the king;" and that
was what Jack did, and they lived in it happily
ever after.

TITTY MOUSE AND TATTY MOUSE

TITTY MOUSE and Tatty Mouse lived in a house, and one day when they were hungry they went out into a wheat field that was near by, and Titty Mouse brought home an ear of wheat and Tatty Mouse brought home an ear of wheat. Titty Mouse took her ear of wheat and picked all the grain out of the husks, and Tatty Mouse took her ear of wheat and picked all the grain out of the husks.

Then Titty Mouse put her wheat in the pot to boil, and Tatty Mouse put her wheat in the pot to boil; and when the wheat was boiled Titty Mouse

was taking the pot off the fire and her foot slipped
and the hot water from the pot splashed on her.
She was scalded so badly that she went to bed sick,
and Tatty sat down and cried.

A three-legged stool saw the tears dropping from
Tatty's eyes, and it asked, "Tatty, why do you
weep?"

"Titty's sick," replied Tatty, "and so I weep."

"Then I'll hop," said the stool. So the stool
hopped.

A broom in the corner of the room saw the stool
hopping and it asked, "Stool, why do you hop?"

"Oh!" replied the stool, "Titty's sick, and
Tatty weeps, and so I hop."

"Then I'll sweep," said the broom. So the
broom began to sweep.

The door saw the broom sweeping and it asked,
"Broom, why do you sweep?"

"Oh!" replied the broom, "Titty's sick,
and Tatty weeps, and the stool hops, and so I
sweep."

"Then I'll creak," said the door. So the door
creaked.

Just outside the door by the house wall stood an
old bench, and when the door creaked the bench
asked, "Door, why do you creak?"

"Oh," replied the door, "Titty's sick, and Tatty weeps, and the stool hops, and the broom sweeps, and so I creak."

"Then I'll run round the house," said the old bench. So the old bench ran round the house.

A fine large walnut-tree grew in the yard and shadowed the house very pleasantly, and when the tree saw the bench running it asked, "Bench, why do you run round the house?"

"Oh!" replied the bench, "Titty's sick, and Tatty weeps, and the stool hops, and the broom sweeps, the door creaks, and so I run round the house."

"Then I'll shed my leaves," said the walnut-tree. So the walnut-tree let fall all its beautiful green leaves.

A little bird was perched on one of the boughs of the tree, and when the leaves all dropped to the ground the bird asked, "Walnut-tree, why do you shed your leaves?"

"Oh!" replied the tree, "Titty's sick, and Tatty weeps, the stool hops, and the broom sweeps, the door creaks, the old bench runs round the house, and so I shed my leaves."

"Then I'll moult all my feathers," said the little bird. So it let fall all its pretty feathers.

When the feathers came drifting down to the ground a little girl happened to be walking along under the tree carrying a pail of milk for her brothers' and sisters' supper. She looked up and asked, " Little bird, why do you drop all your feathers ? "

" Oh ! " replied the little bird, " Titty 's sick, and Tatty weeps, the stool hops, and the broom sweeps, the door creaks, the old bench runs round the house, the walnut-tree sheds its leaves, and so I moult all my feathers."

" Then I 'll spill the milk," said the little girl. So she dropped the pail and spilled the milk.

Not far away an old man was climbing up a ladder to mend the roof of the barn. He saw the little girl drop her pail and he asked, " Little girl what do you mean by spilling the milk ? Your brothers and sisters will now have no milk for their supper."

" Oh ! " replied the little girl, " Titty 's sick, and Tatty weeps, the stool hops, and the broom sweeps, the door creaks, the old bench runs round the house, the walnut-tree sheds its leaves, the little bird moults all its feathers, and so I spill the milk."

" Then I 'll tumble off the ladder," said the old man. So he tumbled off the ladder ; and the little girl was frightened and ran away; and the little bird was frightened and wanted to get away too, but it had moulted all its feathers and when it tried to fly it dropped to the ground. Then the great walnut-tree fell right on the house and smashed it all to pieces; and when the house came down the old bench was upset and the door was knocked out, and the door in falling upset the broom, and the broom fell against the stool and upset that; and poor little Titty Mouse and poor little Tatty Mouse were buried beneath the ruins. But whether they were hurt or not I have never heard said.

THE STORY OF CHICKEN-LICKEN

ONE fine summer morning Chicken-licken went to the woods and an acorn fell from an oak-tree and hit her right on the head. "Gracious me!" said Chicken-liken, "the sky has fallen. I must go and tell the king."

So Chicken-licken turned back, but she had not gone far when she met Hen-len. "Where are you going, Hen-len?" she asked.

"I 'm going to the woods to get something to eat," replied Hen-len.

And Chicken-licken said, "Oh! Hen-len, don't go; for I was going, and the sky fell on my head, and now I 'm going to tell the king."

"I will go with you," said Hen-len.

So Hen-len turned back, and they went along until pretty soon they met Cock-lock. "Where are you going, Cock-lock?" they asked.

"I 'm going to the woods to get something to eat," replied Cock-lock.

Then Hen-len said, " Oh ! Cock-lock, don't go ;
for I was going, and I met Chicken-licken, and
Chicken-licken had been to the woods, and the sky
had fallen on her head, and we are going to tell
the king."

" I will go with you," said Cock-lock.

So Cock-lock turned back and they went along
until pretty soon they met Ducky-daddles.
" Where are you going, Ducky-daddles ? " they
asked.

" I 'm going to the woods to get something to
eat," replied Ducky-daddles.

Then Cock-lock said, " Oh ! Ducky-daddles,
don't go ; for I was going, and I met Hen-len, and
Hen-len had met Chicken-licken, and Chicken-
licken had been to the woods and the sky had
fallen on her head, and we are going to tell the
king."

" I will go with you," said Ducky-daddles.

So Ducky-daddles turned back and they went
along until pretty soon they met Goosie-poosie.
" Where are you going, Goosie-poosie ? " they asked.

" I 'm going to the woods to get something to
eat," replied Goosie-poosie.

Then Ducky-daddles said, "Oh! Goosie-poosie,
don't go ; for I was going, and I met Cock-lock,

and Cock-lock had met Hen-len, and Hen-len had
met Chicken-licken, and Chicken-licken had been
to the woods and the sky had fallen on her head,
and we are going to tell the king."

" I will go with you," said Goosie-poosie.

So Goosie-poosie turned back and they went
along until pretty soon they met Turkey-lurkey.
" Where are you going, Turkey-lurkey ? " they
asked.

"I'm going to the woods to get something to
eat," replied Turkey-lurkey.

Then Goosie-poosie said, " Oh ! Turkey-lurkey,
don't go ; for I was going, and I met Ducky-daddles,
and Ducky-daddles had met Cock-lock, and Cock-
lock had met Hen-len, and Hen-len had met
Chicken-licken, and Chicken-licken had been to
the woods and the sky had fallen on her head, and
we are going to tell the king."

" I will go with you," said Turkey-lurkey.

So Turkey-lurkey turned back and they went
along until pretty soon they met Fox-lox ; and
Fox-lox said, " Where are you going, my pretty
dears ? "

And they replied, " Chicken-licken went to the
woods and the sky fell on her head, and we are
going to tell the king."

"All right," said Fox-lox, "come along with me, and I will show you the way."

So they went along with Fox-lox, and he took them to his hole, and he and his young ones soon ate up poor Chicken-licken, Hen-len, Cock-lock, Ducky-daddles, Goosie-poosie, and Turkey-lurkey, and they never saw the king to tell him that the sky had fallen.

KING O'TOOLE AND HIS GOOSE

IN Ireland there was once a king called King
O'Toole, and he was very fond of hunting.
Up he got every morning at the rising of
the sun, and away he went over the mountains
after the deer. As long as he had his health this
kind of life just suited King O'Toole; but in the
course of time he grew old and was stiff in his
limbs, and could go hunting no more. Then the
king was very sad, and at last he got a goose which
he hoped might divert him somewhat.

The goose did its best, and it used to fly about
over the lake near the king's castle and swim in
the water and dive and catch fish. The king liked
to watch the goose, and for a considerable time it
entertained him very well; but at last the goose
got stricken in years like its master, and could not
divert him any longer. Then King O'Toole felt
so downhearted that life seemed to him scarcely
worth living. One morning he was walking by

the lake lamenting his unhappy fate, and thinking
he might as well drown himself when he met a
young man.

" God save you," said the king.

" God save you kindly, King O'Toole," said the
young man, who was none other that Saint Kavin
in disguise.

" I have never seen you before," said the king.
" Who are you ? "

" I 'm an honest man," replied Saint Kavin.

" Well, honest man," said the king, " you wear
good clothing and look prosperous and as if you
had money laid by.   How do you get your living,
may I ask ? "

" By making old things as good as new," was
Saint Kavin's reply.

" Is it a tinker you are ? " inquired the king.

" No," responded the saint.   " I'm not a tinker.
I 've a better trade than that ; and what would you
say, King O'Toole, if I made your old goose young
again ? "

At the thought of having his old goose young
once more the king's eyes were ready to jump out of
his head.   Then he whistled, and the old goose
came waddling to him from behind a clump of
bushes near by.

The minute the saint set eyes on the goose he took pity on its feebleness and said, " I 'll do the job for you, King O'Toole."

" Bedad ! " exclaimed the king, " if you do I 'll say you are the cleverest fellow in siven parishes."

" But you 'll have to say more than that," was

Saint Kavin's response. " I 'm not going to repair your old goose for nothing, and I want to know how much you 're going to give me."

" I 'll give you whatever you ask," said the king. " Is n't that fair ? "

" Yes, yes," said Saint Kavin, " that 's the way to do business. Now this is the bargain I 'll make

with you, King O'Toole — you give me all the
ground the goose goes over in its first flight after
I make it young and strong."

"Done !" said the king.

"Well, then," continued Saint Kavin, "I'll go to
work at once," and he called the old goose to him
and took it up by its two wings. "Criss o' my
cross on you," said he and threw the bird up into
the air — and how the goose did fly ! It went swift
and high and cut as many capers as a swallow before
a shower of rain.

The king stood with his mouth open watching
with delight the bird's every motion, and when it
came and lit at his feet he patted it on the head and
said, " My dear, you are the darlint of the world."

But the goose in its flight had covered a great
deal of country. It had been over the castle and
all the king's land for a mile around. "And now
what have you to say to me for makin' your goose
like that?" asked Saint Kavin.

"I'm very much beholden to you," replied the
king.

" And will you give me all the ground the goose
flew over?" Saint Kavin inquired.

"I will," said King O'Toole, "and you'd be
welcome to it even if it took the last acre I had."

"And you 'll keep your word true?" questioned the saint.

"Of course I will," affirmed the king.

"It 's well for you, King O'Toole, that you speak as you do," declared Saint Kavin; "for ·if you did not keep your promise I 'd never let your goose fly again."

"Waste no more words!" exclaimed King O'Toole, "the land is yours."

"But I don't want your land," said Saint Kavin. "I only came here to try you, and you 're a very dacint man, King O'Toole; and now I 'll tell you that I 'm disguised, and that is the reason you do not know me."

"Musha! then," said the king, "and who might you be?"

"I 'm Saint Kavin," was the reply.

"Oh, queen of heaven!" the king exclaimed, falling on his knees before the saint, "is it the great Saint Kavin I 've been discoursing with all this time?"

"It is," said the saint.

"Be jabers! I thought I was only talking to a lump of a gossoon!" said the king.

"Well, you know the difference now," remarked the good saint.

And so King O'Toole had his goose made young again to divert him as long as he lived. But by and by the king died, and soon afterward the goose got into trouble with a big eel in the lake. The goose was fishing and got hold of the eel by mistake, and, instead of the goose killing the eel, the eel killed the goose. However, the eel did not eat the goose, for it did not dare eat what Saint Kavin had laid his blessed hands on.

THE THREE LITTLE PIGS

ONCE upon a time there was an old mother pig and three little pigs and they lived in the middle of an oak forest. While the children were still quite small the acorn crop failed. That made it difficult for Mrs. Piggy-wiggy to find enough for her children to eat, and the little pigs had to go hungry. So at last the mother pig sent the little pigs off to seek their fortunes.

The first little pig to go walked on and on until he met a man carrying a bundle of straw, and the little pig said, " Please, man, give me that straw to build me a house."

So the man gave the little pig the straw, and the little pig built a house of it. In this house of straw the little pig lived very comfortably ; but one day a wolf came along and rapped at the door. " Little pig, little pig, let me come in," said the wolf.

" No, no, by the hair of my chinny, chin, chin," said the little pig.

" Then I 'll huff and I 'll puff and I 'll blow your house down," said the wolf.

So he huffed and he puffed and he blew the house down and carried the little pig off to his den.

The second little pig that left the mother pig walked on and on until he met a man carrying a bundle of brush, and the little pig said, " Please, man, give me that brush to build me a house."

So the man gave the little pig the brush, and the little pig built a house of it. In this house of brush the little pig lived very comfortably ; but one day the wolf came along and rapped at the door. " Little pig, little pig, let me come in," said the wolf.

" No, no, by the hair of my chinny, chin, chin," said the little pig.

" Then I 'll huff and I 'll puff and I 'll blow your house down," said the wolf.

So he huffed and he puffed, and he puffed and he huffed, and at last he blew the house down and carried off the little pig.

The third little pig, after he left the mother pig, walked on and on until he met a man with a load of bricks, and the little pig said, " Please, man, give me those bricks to build me a house."

So the man gave the little pig the bricks and the little pig built a house of them. In this house of bricks the little pig lived very comfortably; but one day the wolf came along and rapped at the door. "Little pig, little pig, let me come in," said the wolf.

"No, no, by the hair of my chinny, chin, chin," said the little pig.

"Then I'll huff and I'll puff and I'll blow your house down," said the wolf.

So he huffed and he puffed, and he huffed and he puffed, and he puffed and he huffed; but the house was built of bricks and he could not blow it down. At last he had no breath left to huff and puff with, so he sat down outside the little pig's house and thought for a while. Presently he said, "Little pig, I know where there is a nice field of turnips."

"Where?" asked the little pig.

"Not half a mile from here, at Farmer Smith's," replied the wolf. "If you will be ready to-morrow morning I will call for you and we will go together and get some turnips for dinner."

"At what time do you mean to go?" said the little pig.

"Oh, at six o'clock," the wolf answered.

"Very well," said the little pig, "I will be ready."

But the little pig got up at *five* o'clock and he went off to Farmer Smith's and filled a basket with turnips and returned home before the wolf came. He had locked the door and was busy about his housework when he heard the wolf rapping outside.

"Little pig, are you ready?" the wolf said.

"Ready!" exclaimed the little pig, "I have been to the turnip field and got back, and I'm paring the turnips for dinner now."

The wolf was very angry at this, but he was bound to catch the little pig in some way or other. So he thought a moment and then he said, "Little pig, I know where there is a nice apple-tree loaded with apples."

"Where?" asked the little pig.

"Down in the valley at Farmer Brown's," replied the wolf. "If you will be ready to-morrow morning I will call for you at five o'clock and we will go together and get some apples for dinner."

"Very well," said the little pig, "I will be ready."

But the next morning the little pig was up at *four* o'clock and he hurried down to Farmer Brown's in the valley. He hoped to return home before the wolf arrived; but he had farther to go than the day before, and he had to climb the tree to fill the bag he had brought with the apples. So the wolf got to the little pig's house while the little pig was gone for the apples, and found the house empty. Then the wolf ran to Farmer Brown's as fast as he could go, and when he came to the apple-tree the little pig was just preparing to climb down from among the branches.

" Little pig," said the wolf, " you treat me very badly. You should have waited for me."

The little pig was much frightened, but he said, " These are splendid apples. I will throw you down one ; " and he threw the apple so far that while the wolf was gone to pick it up the little pig jumped to the ground and ran home.

Early the next day the wolf came to the little pig's house again and said, " Little pig, there is a fair at the town in the valley this afternoon. Will you go ? "

" Oh, yes," replied the little pig. " I will go. At what time do you want to start ? "

" At three," said the wolf.

But the little pig went off before the time, as usual, and got to the fair and bought a churn. He was carrying the churn home when he saw the wolf coming. Then he could not tell what to do. So

he crawled into the churn to hide.   But he happened
to be near the top of a hill, and no sooner was he
in the churn than it began to roll and bump down

the hill with the little pig squealing and kicking
inside ; for he was badly scared and thought he
would be bumped to death, or, if not that, he was
sure the wolf would get him.

The wolf, however, imagined the churn was some

strange beast that meant him harm.   He had never
seen or heard the like in all his life, and he was so
terrified he turned about and ran home without
going to the fair.   He did not venture out again
till toward evening.   Then he went to the little
pig's house and said, " Little pig, did you go to
the fair ? "

" Oh, yes," said the little pig, " I went to the fair,
and why did n't you go ? "

" I started to go," replied the wolf, " but when
I was nearly there a great howling round thing
chased me.   It had its mouth wide open and could
easily have swallowed me whole.   I had to run with
all my might or it would have caught me."

" Ha, ha ! " laughed the little pig, " it was I who
frightened you.   I had been to the fair and bought
a churn, and when I saw you I crawled into it and
rolled down the hill."

Then the wolf was so angry that he declared
he would eat up the little pig without any more
delay.   " You can't keep me out, even if you have
locked the door," shouted the wolf.   " I will come
down the chimney ! "

The little pig had a big pot of water boiling on
the fire, and when he heard the wolf scrambling up
the roof he took the cover off the pot.   A minute

later the wolf came down the chimney and fell right into the pot, and the little pig put the cover on and that was the last of the wicked wolf. After that the little pig lived very happily in his house of bricks and there he is to this day.

14

THE FAIRY COW

THERE was once an old woman whose home was a poor little cottage in a country village. She got a living by doing odd jobs for the farmers' wives round about. It was not much she could earn, yet, with a silver piece here and a few pennies there, and sometimes the gift of a bit of meat, or a little tea, she contrived to get along without serious discomfort, and she was as cheerful as if she had not a want in the world.

One summer evening as she was going home she came on a stout, black pot lying at the side of the road. "Now who could have left that pot here?" said she, looking about to see if any one was in sight to whom it might belong. "It would be just the very thing for me," she continued, "if I had something to put in it. But stop! maybe it has been thrown away and has a hole in the bottom. Ah, yes! that is the trouble, I'll be bound. Still, the hole would not prevent the pot doing fine to put some flowers in for the window, and I'm thinking I'll take it home any way."

So she bent her stiff old back and lifted the lid to look inside. But what she saw so surprised her that she jumped back to the middle of the road, exclaiming, " Mercy me! the pot is full to the brim of gold pieces. Who would have thought it!"

For a while she could do nothing but walk round and round her treasure, admiring the yellow gold and wondering at her good fortune and saying over and over, " Well, I do be feeling rich and grand."

Presently, however, she picked up the pot and started again toward home. " No one will see what I'm taking along with me," said she; " for the sun is gone and it is growing dark, and I'll have all the night to myself to think what I'll do with this mass of golden money. I could buy a fine house with it and live like the queen herself and not do a stroke of work, but just sit comfortable by the fire all day with a cup of tea; or maybe I'll go to the minister and ask him to keep the money for me, and then I'd get a little of it from him every week as I was wanting; or perhaps I'll bury it in a hole in the garden and only save out one or two pieces to put on the mantel between my china teapot and the candles for ornament, you know. Ah! I feel so grand I don't know myself rightly!"

By this time she had become rather tired with

carrying such a heavy weight and she stopped to
rest. She set the pot down and then thought
she would have another look at her wealth. But
when she took the cover off she saw that instead of
gold the pot was full of shining silver. She stared
and rubbed her eyes and stared again.

"I would have sworn it was gold," she said;
"but I reckon I must have been dreaming. Well,
whatever it was I'm better off with silver than gold.
It'll be far less trouble to look after, and not so
likely to be stolen. Those gold pieces would have
made a sight of bother to keep 'em safe. Yes, yes,
I'm well quit of them, and with the pot full of silver
I'm as rich as any one need be."

Then she set off homeward again cheerfully
planning all the things she was going to do with
her money. But by and by she grew tired once
more and paused to rest for a minute or two; and
of course she had to have another look into the
pot. As soon as she took off the cover she cried
out in amazement, for there was nothing inside but
a lump of iron. "Well, well!" she cried, "that
does beat all! and yet how nice it is to have such a
fine heavy piece of iron. I can sell it easy, and the
pennies it brings will come very handy. Ah, yes,
it is far better to have this iron than a lot of gold or

silver that would have kept me from sleeping nights thinking bad men would be prowling around to rob me. Oh, I am doing very well indeed!"

On she went, now, pot in hand, chuckling to herself over her good fortune until her arm was tired of the burden, and for the third time she set the pot down that she might rest and have another glance at its contents. She took off the cover and peeped in and was astonished to find nought except a stone. "Deary me!" she said, "a stone is it this time! Yes, yes, and glad I am to have it. I 've been wanting a stone like that to hold my door open with. It will be the very thing! Ah, did any one ever hear of such fine luck as mine!"

She was in haste to see how the stone would look in the corner by her door, and she hurried on until she came to her cottage gate. In order to unfasten the gate she put the pot down, and when she stooped to pick it up she heard something inside and took the cover off. Instantly out leaped an animal that grew in a moment into a big cow, and the pot disappeared. The cow shook its legs and flourished its tail and bellowed and laughed and ran off kicking its feet into the air.

The old woman gazed after it in speechless bewilderment till it was fairly out of sight. " Well," she said at last, " I surely am the luckiest body hereabouts. Fancy my seeing a fairy cow all to myself, and making so free with it too !   I never in all my life felt so grand ! "

Then she went into her cottage and sat down by the fire to think over her good luck.

THE MASTER OF ALL MASTERS

A GIRL once hired herself for a servant to a queer old gentleman who, as soon as she came to his house ready for work, said, "Before you begin I want to give you some instructions."

"Very well, sir," said she.

"In my house I have my own names for things," he continued, "and I beg you to carefully heed and remember what I say."

"Oh, certainly, sir, I will do that," she replied.

"Now, firstly," said he, "what will you call me?"

"Oh, I will call you master, or mister, or whatever you please, sir," said she.

"No, no," said he, "you must call me 'master of all masters'; and what would you call this?" he asked pointing to his bed.

"Oh, I would call it a bed, or a couch, or whatever you please, sir," she replied.

"No," said he, "that's my 'barnacle'; and what

do you call these?" he inquired, pointing to his pantaloons.

"Oh, I call them breeches, or trousers, or whatever you please, sir," said she.

"You must call them 'squibs and crackers,'" said he; "and what would you call her?" he asked, pointing to the cat.

"Oh, I would call her cat, or pussy, or whatever you please, sir," said she.

"You must call her 'white-faced simminy,'" said he; "and what do you call this?" he asked, waving his hand toward the fire.

"Oh, I call it fire, or flame, or whatever you please, sir," said she.

"You must call it 'hot cockalorum,'" said he; "and what do you call this?" he asked, pointing to some water.

"Oh, I call it water, or wet, or whatever you please, sir," she replied.

"No," said he, "'pondybus' is its name here; and what do you call the building in which I reside?"

"Oh, I call it house, or cottage, or whatever you please, sir," said she.

"You must call it 'high-topper mountain,'" he ordered.

That very night the servant awoke her master

from a sound sleep by pounding with her fists on his door and shouting in great fright, " Master of all masters, get out of your barnacle and put on your squibs and crackers ; for white-faced simminy has got a spark of hot cockalorum on her tail, and un-less you get some pondybus, the high-topper mountain will be all on hot cockalorum!"

In saying this she had used just the words her master had ordered, but by so doing she had been so long explaining what was the matter that the house was on fire by the time she finished.   The flames spread rapidly, and though the servant and her master escaped, the building burned to the ground.

The queer old gentleman built another house presently and hired another servant; but he let her call things by their ordinary names, and did not attempt to teach her invented ones of his own.

MR. MICRAWBLE

TOMMY TODKINS was sometimes a good boy and sometimes a bad boy; and when he was a bad boy he was a *very* bad boy. On stormy days his mother used to say to him, "Now, Tommy, don't go out on the street until it stops raining."

"But I want to go," said Tommy.

"No, you would get wet and be sick, I'm afraid," replied his mother, "and besides Mr. Micrawble might catch you."

Yet when Tommy was a bad boy he would go out on the street in spite of what his mother said, no matter if it did rain; and one day, sure enough, Mr. Micrawble caught him and popped him in a bag upside down and carried him off.

As soon as Mr. Micrawble reached home he pulled Tommy out of the bag and felt of his arms and legs. "You're rather lean," said he. "However, you're all the meat I've got for supper and it's high time I had you boiling in the pot — but dear me! I've

forgotten to get the potatoes and turnips and oth
vegetables.   You 'd not taste good alone."

Then he called to Mrs. Micrawble, "Sally.
Here, I say, Sally !"

So Mrs. Micrawble came and asked, "What do
you want, my dear?"

"Oh, I 've caught a little boy for supper," replied Mr. Micrawble, "but I 've forgotten the
vegetables.   Look after him, will you, while I go
for them?"

"All right," said Mrs. Micrawble, and off he
went.

Then Tommy Todkins said to Mrs. Micrawble,
"Does Mr. Micrawble always have little boys for
supper?"

"Yes, mostly," answered Mrs. Micrawble; "for
if the little boys are bad enough and get in his way
he 's sure to catch them."

"And don't you have anything else but boy-meat
— no pudding?"   Tommy inquired.

"Ah! I love pudding," said Mrs. Micrawble;
"but it 's very seldom, indeed, that I get it."

"Why! my mother is making a pudding this
very day," said Tommy, "and she 'd give you some
of it if I asked her.   Shall I run and get some?"

"Now, that 's a thoughtful boy," responded Mrs.

..icrawble. "You can go, only don't stay long,
..id be sure to get back for supper."

So Tommy ran home as fast as he could go, but
he did not think it was safe to return with the pudding for Mrs. Micrawble. Many a long day passed
and Tommy was as good as good could be, and
never went out to play on rainy days. However,

it was very hard to be always good, and finally he ventured out one wet afternoon, and, as luck would have it, Mr. Micrawble happened along and picked Tommy Todkins up and carried him off once more in his bag.

When Mr. Micrawble got home and shook Tommy out of the bag and had a look at him he said, "Ah, you're the youngster that served me and my wife such a shabby trick a while ago, and left us without any supper. Well, you sha'n't do that again. Here, get under the sofa, and I'll sit on it and watch till the pot boils for you."

So poor Tommy Todkins had to crawl under the sofa, and Mr. Micrawble sat on it and waited for the pot to boil; and he waited and he waited and he waited, but still the pot did not boil. Then Mrs. Micrawble went out to chop some wood for the fire, and Mr. Micrawble fell asleep.

"Now, I must get away from here," said Tommy to himself when he heard Mr. Micrawble snoring, and he crept out from under the sofa and was stepping softly along toward the door when he saw Mrs. Micrawble coming across the yard with her arms full of wood. He was too late to escape in that direction and he looked around for a place to hide. The door of the brick oven at the side of the fireplace was open, and by standing on a chair he got up to it and crawled in. Then he pulled the door closed, but the door creaked and awakened Mr. Micrawble.

"What was that I heard?" said Mr. Micrawble, and he looked under the sofa to see if Tommy was still there. "Sally, my dear Sally!" he called just as his wife came in with the wood, "that boy has gone!"

"Well, I have been in the yard all the time," said Mrs. Micrawble, "and he could n't have come from the house without my seeing him. Perhaps he went upstairs."

"Yes," said Mr. Micrawble, "he must have gone upstairs. We will go up and find him."

But as soon as Tommy Todkins heard their footsteps going up the stairs he climbed out of the oven and hurried home. After that he did not go onto the street to play when it stormed, and Mr. Micrawble never caught him again.

THE FISHERMAN AND HIS WIFE

THERE was once a fisherman who lived with his wife in a poor little hut close by the sea. One day, as the fisherman sat on the rocks at the water's edge fishing with his rod and line, a fish got caught on his hook that was so big and pulled so stoutly that he captured it with the greatest difficulty. He was feeling much pleased that he had secured so big a fish when he was surprised by hearing it say to him, " Pray let me live. 1 am not a real fish. I am a magician. Put me in the water and let me go."

" You need not make so many words about the matter," said the man. " I wish to have nothing to do with a fish that can talk."

Then he removed it from his hook and put it back into the water. " Now swim away as soon as you please," said the man, and the fish darted straight down to the bottom.

The fisherman returned to his little hut and told his wife how he had caught a great fish, and how it

had told him it was a magician, and how, when he
heard it speak, he had let it go.

"Did you not ask it for anything?" said the wife.

"No," replied the man; "what should I ask
for?"

"What should you ask for!" exclaimed the wife,

"You talk as if we had everything we want, but see how wretchedly we live in this dark little hut. Do go back and tell the fish we want a comfortable house."

The fisherman did not like to undertake such an errand. However, as his wife had bidden him to go, he went; and when he came to the sea the water looked all yellow and green. He stood on the rocks where he had fished and said,

"Oh, man of the sea!
Come listen to me;
For Alice my wife,
The plague of my life,
Hath sent me to beg a gift of thee!"

Then the fish came swimming to him and said, "Well, what does she want?"

"Ah," answered the fisherman, "my wife says that when I had caught you I ought to have asked you for something before I let you go. She does not like living any longer in our little hut. She wants a comfortable house."

"Go home then," said the fish; "she is in the house she wants already."

So the man went home and found his wife standing in the doorway of a comfortable house, and behind the house was a yard with ducks and

chickens picking about in it, and beyond the yard
was a garden where grew all sorts of flowers and

fruits. "How happily we shall live now!" said
the fisherman.

Everything went right for a week or two, and
then the wife said, "Husband, there is not enough
room in this house, and the yard and garden are a
great deal smaller than they ought to be. I would

like to have a large stone castle to live in.   So go to
the fish again and tell him to give us a castle."

"Wife," said the fisherman, "I don't like
to go to him again, for perhaps he will be angry.
We ought to be content with a good house like
this."

"Nonsense!" said the wife, "he will give us a
castle very willingly.   Go along and try."

The fisherman went, but his heart was heavy,
and when he came to the sea the water was a dark
gray color and looked very gloomy.   He stood on
the rocks at the water's edge and said,

> "Oh, man of the sea!
>   Come listen to me;
>   For Alice my wife,
>   The plague of my life,
> Hath sent me to beg a gift of thee!"

Then the fish came swimming to him and said,
"Well, what does she want now?"

"Ah," replied the man very sorrowfully, "my
wife wants to live in a stone castle."

"Go home then," said the fish; "she is at the
castle already."

So away went the fisherman and found his wife
standing before a great castle.   "See," said she, "is
not this fine?"

They went into the castle, and many servants were there, and the rooms were richly furnished with handsome chairs and tables; and behind the castle was a park half a mile long, full of sheep and goats and rabbits and deer.

"Now," said the man, "we will live contented and happy in this beautiful castle for the rest of our lives."

"Perhaps so," responded the wife; "but let us consider and sleep on it before we make up our minds," and they went to bed.

The next morning when they awoke it was broad daylight, and the wife jogged the fisherman with her elbow and said, "Get up, husband; bestir yourself, for we must be king and queen of all the land."

"Wife, wife," said the man, "why should we wish to be king and queen? I would not be king even if I could be."

"Well, I will be queen, anyway," said the wife. "Say no more about it; but go to the fish and tell him what I want."

So the man went, but he felt very sad to think that his wife should want to be queen. The sea was muddy and streaked with foam as he cried out,

"Oh, man of the sea !
Come listen to me ;
For Alice my wife,
The plague of my life,
Hath sent me to beg a gift of thee ! "

Then the fish came swimming to him and said, "Well, what would she have now?"

"Alas!" said the man, "my wife wants to be queen."

"Go home," said the fish; "she is queen already."

So the fisherman turned back and presently he came to a palace, and before it he saw a troop of soldiers, and he heard the sound of drums and trumpets. Then he entered the palace and there he found his wife sitting on a throne, with a golden crown on her head, and on each side of her stood six beautiful maidens.

"Well, wife," said the fisherman, "are you queen?"

"Yes," she replied, "I am queen."

When he had looked at her for a long time he said, "Ah, wife ! what a fine thing it is to be queen ! Now we shall never have anything more to wish for."

"I don't know how that may be," said she; "never is a long time. I am queen, 't is true, but I begin to be tired of it. I think I would like to be pope next."

"Oh, wife, wife!" the man exclaimed, "how can you be pope? There is but one pope at a time in all Christendom."

"Husband," said she, "I will be pope this very day."

"Ah, wife!" responded the fisherman, "the fish cannot make you pope and I would not like to ask for such a thing."

"What nonsense!" said she. "If he can make a queen, he can make a pope. Go and try."

So the fisherman went, and when he came to the shore the wind was raging and the waves were dashing on the rocks most fearfully, and the sky was dark with flying clouds. The fisherman was frightened, but nevertheless he obeyed his wife and called out,

> "Oh, man of the sea!
> Come listen to me;
> For Alice my wife,
> The plague of my life,
> Hath sent me to beg a gift of thee!"

Then the fish came swimming to him and said, "What does she want this time?"

"Ah!" said the fisherman, "my wife wants to be pope."

"Go home," commanded the fish; "she is pope already."

So the fisherman went home and found his wife sitting on a throne that was a hundred feet high, and on either side many candles of all sizes were burning, and she had three great crowns on her head one above the other and was surrounded by all the pomp and power of the Church.

"Wife," said the fisherman, as he gazed at all this magnificence, "are you pope?"

"Yes," she replied, "I am pope."

"Well, wife," said he, "it is a grand thing to be pope; and now you must be content, for you can be nothing greater."

"We will see about that," she said.

Then they went to bed; but the wife could not sleep because all night long she was trying to think what she should be next. At last morning came and the sun rose. "Ha!" cried she, "I was about to sleep, had not the sun disturbed me with its bright light. Cannot I prevent the sun rising?" and she became very angry and said to her husband, "Go to the fish and tell him I want to be lord of the sun and moon."

"Alas, wife!" said he, "can you not be content to be pope?"

"No," said she, "I am very uneasy, and cannot bear to see the sun and moon rise without my leave. Go to the fish at once!"

The man went, and as he approached the shore a dreadful storm arose so that the trees and rocks shook, and the sky grew black, and the lightning flashed, and the thunder rolled, and the sea was covered with vast waves like mountains. The fisherman trembled so that his knees knocked together, and he had hardly strength to stand in the gale while he called to the fish:

> " Oh, man of the sea!
>   Come listen to me ;
>   For Alice my wife,
>   The plague of my life,
>   Hath sent me to beg a gift of thee! "

Then the fish came swimming to him and said, " What more does she want ? "

" Ah ! " said the man, " she wants to be lord of the sun and moon."

" Go home to your hut again," said the fish.

So the man returned, and the palace was gone, and in its place he found the dark little hut that had formerly been his dwelling, and he and his wife have lived in that little hut to this very day.

CINDERELLA

ONCE upon a time there was a girl whose father and mother had died, and she had gone to live with a family of wealthy relatives. They did not like to be burdened with her and they treated her very badly, though she was the sweetest, best-tempered creature that ever was.

The lady of the house was proud and disagreeable, and she had two daughters who were very much like her. They made their poor relative work in the kitchen and do all the household drudgery. It was she who washed the dishes and scrubbed down the stairs and swept the floors. She had to sleep in the garret on a wretched bed of straw, while the rooms of the two sisters were very elegant, and were furnished with nice feather-beds and had full-length looking-glasses in which the young ladies could admire themselves all day long.

The poor girl bore her troubles with patience and never complained. When she had finished her day's work she used to sit in the chimney-corner on a low stool among the ashes and cinders, and so the sisters nicknamed her Cinderella. But Cinderella, in spite of hard work and shabby clothes, was a hundred times prettier than they were, decked out in all their finery.

It happened after a time that the king's son gave a grand ball which was to continue for two nights and to which he invited all persons of fashion for miles around; and as the two young ladies made a great figure in society they, of course, received invitations. "We shall certainly go," said they, " and perhaps we may have the chance to dance with the prince."

So they were wonderfully busy choosing such dresses as might be most becoming, and could talk of nothing but their fine clothes day in and day out. " I shall put on my red velvet dress with point lace trimmings," said the elder.

"And I," said the younger sister, "shall wear my gold-brocaded train and my circlet of diamonds."

Their preparations made no end of trouble for Cinderella, and she was kept constantly engaged in plaiting ruffles, sewing, arranging bows and ribbons, and in washing and ironing the sisters' linen. But she helped willingly all she could, and when the great day came, offered to dress the young ladies' hair. They were glad to have her do that, and while she was brushing and combing they said to her, " Cinderella, would not you like to go to the ball ? "

" Yes," said she, " but so grand a ball as this is to be is not for such as I am."

" You are quite right," they said, " for every one would laugh to see a ragged kitchen girl there."

Cinderella finished the young ladies' hair and assisted them to dress, and they never before in their lives had been arrayed half so becomingly. Indeed, they were so delighted that at dinner-time they could scarcely eat a morsel; and, besides, it was not easy to eat much, for they had laced very tight to make their waists as slender as possible.

What they had said to Cinderella about the ball set her to thinking how nice it would be if she really could attend it, and finally she asked the sisters' mother, who chanced to come into the kitchen while she was washing the dinner dishes, to let her go.

" You, Cinderella ! " exclaimed the lady. " Why! you are wearing the only dress you have — and just look at it ! What could put such an idea into your head ? But, see here," said she, taking up a dish of peas that was on a shelf, " I will throw this basinful of peas into the ash-heap behind the house, and if you can get every pea picked out of the ashes in an hour's time you can go to the ball with my daughters."

Then the lady, followed by Cinderella, carried the peas out and threw them into the ashes. "Here is the basin," said she, handing it to the girl, "and you can go at your task as soon as you choose."

She returned to the house, and Cinderella stood looking at the ash-heap. "I could not find all those peas in a week's time," said she; "I must have help." And she began to call,

> "Hither, hither, through the sky,
> All you little songsters fly!
> One and all, come help me quick,
> Make haste, make haste — come pick, pick, pick!"

At once a great number of little birds came chirping and fluttering to the ash-heap and commenced to pick, pick, pick. Cinderella held the basin and they brought the peas one by one and dropped them into it. In a short time she had all the peas out of the ashes and carried them in to her mistress overjoyed at the thought she could now go to the ball. But the lady said, "No, no, you haven't clothes. I spoke in jest before. You shall not go; for you would only put us to shame."

Evening came and the two young women set off

for the ball, and Cinderella watched them until they were out of sight and then stood by the fire and wept. At this moment a good fairy appeared and asked her what was the matter.

" I wish — I wish — " began the poor girl, but her voice was choked with tears.

" You wish that you could go to the ball," interrupted the fairy.

" Indeed I do," said Cinderella, with a sigh.

" Well, then, stop crying," said the fairy, " and I think I can contrive to have you go not only this evening, but to-morrow evening, too. Run into the garden and bring me a pumpkin."

Cinderella hurried out and brought back the finest pumpkin she could find, though she could not imagine what the fairy wanted of it. But the fairy took a knife, scooped out the pumpkin quite hollow an' touched it with her wand. Immediately it was changed into a splendid carriage. " Now," said the fairy, " is n't there a mouse-trap set in the store-room ? "

" Yes," replied Cinderella.

" Go and see if there are any mice in it," the fairy ordered.

Cinderella soon returned, bringing the trap with six mice inside. " Lift the trap door a little and let

them out," said the fairy, and as the mice escaped
from the trap she changed each one by a stroke of
her wand into a fine dapple-gray horse.

" But what shall we do for a coachman ? " asked
the fairy.

"There's likely to be a rat in the trap in the cellar if you could make a coachman out of him," suggested Cinderella.

"That's a good thought," the fairy responded. "So look at the trap without delay."

Cinderella was quickly back with the trap, and in it was a rat with a tremendous pair of whiskers. The fairy touched the rat with her wand and it became a fat jolly coachman with the smartest whiskers ever seen.

"The next thing for you to do," said the fairy to Cinderella, "is to go again to the garden. You will find two lizards behind the watering-pot. Bring them."

The lizards were no sooner brought than the fairy turned them into footmen with laced liveries, and they skipped up to a seat at the back of the coach just as naturally as if they had been footmen all their lives.

"Well," said the fairy, "here is your coach and six horses, your coachman and your footmen to take you to the ball. Are you not pleased?"

"Oh, yes!" replied Cinderella, "but must I go in these shabby clothes?"

The fairy smiled and tapped her with her wand, when her rags were changed to a dress of cloth of

gold all decked with costly jewels. This done, she
gave her a pair of the prettiest slippers in the world,
made of glass.

"These slippers," said she, "I give you to keep
always, but the other things are enchanted into the
forms they have at present for only a short time."

Cinderella now got into the carriage, and as she
was about to start the fairy said, "Do not on any
account stay after midnight, for if you do the coach
will be a pumpkin again, your horses mice, your
coachman a rat, your footmen lizards, and your
beautiful clothes the rags you wear every day."

Cinderella promised the fairy she would not
fail to leave the ball before midnight, and drove
away in an ecstasy of delight. When she arrived
at the palace the guards and attendants were so
struck by her magnificent equipage that they supposed her to be some rich princess. At once the
carriage was surrounded by courtiers who assisted
her to alight and conducted her to the ball-room.
The moment she appeared all voices were hushed,
the violins ceased playing, and the dancing stopped
short. Everybody was admiring the stranger's
beauty. "How handsome she is! How sur-
passingly lovely!" and similar expressions were
heard on all sides, and the old king whispered to

the queen that he had not seen so comely a young woman in many a long day.

All the ladies busied themselves in considering her clothes and head-dress, that they might have garments of the same pattern, provided they could find such rich materials and seamstresses capable of making them up. The prince came forward to receive Cinderella, and he so admired her beauty and manners that he promptly offered her his hand to dance. Cinderella, pleased beyond measure at this gracious reception and at the splendor of all she saw, danced with the greatest animation. The proud sisters, in whose home she lived, were vexed to have any one attract more attention than themselves; but they did not recognize the ragged kitchen girl in the superb garments she now wore.

A fine supper was presently served, and the young prince helped Cinderella to every delicacy, but was so taken up with gazing at the fair stranger that he did not eat anything himself. Time passed fast, and she never looked at the clock until it was a quarter to twelve. Immediately she rose, made a low courtesy to the whole assembly, and retired in haste. Her carriage was ready at the door of the palace and she jumped into it and drove home as fast as she could.

When she reached the house the coach, horses,

and servants all disappeared and Cinderella found herself clothed in her old ragged gown. She waited beside the fire for the return of the sisters, eager to know what they would say; but she determined to tell them nothing of her own experiences. At length they came knocking at the door, and when Cinderella let them in she pretended to yawn, and rubbed her eyes, saying, "How late you are!" just as if she had been waked out of a nap.

"You would not have thought it late if you had been at the ball," said one of the sisters, "and seen the beautiful princess who was there."

"What princess was she?" asked Cinderella. "What was her name?"

"We do not know her name," was the reply; "nor does anybody, and the king's son would give a fortune to learn who she is."

"If she is so beautiful as all that, how I would like to see her!" exclaimed Cinderella. "Oh, my Lady Charlotte," said she, addressing the elder sister, "do lend me the yellow dress you wear every day, that I may put it on and go to the ball to-morrow evening and have a peep at this wonderful princess."

"What! lend my clothes to a common kitchen girl like you!" cried Miss Charlotte, "I would n't think of such a thing."

Cinderella expected to be refused, and was not sorry, for she would have been very much puzzled what to do had the yellow dress really been lent to her.

On the following evening the sisters again went to the court ball, and shortly after their departure the good fairy came to Cinderella and told her to prepare to go also. A touch of the fairy's wand served to clothe Cinderella even more richly than she had been clothed on the previous occasion. The equipage she had used the night before conveyed her to the palace, and she was ushered into the ball-room with every attention. The prince was rejoiced to see her and never once left her side the evening through. He talked so charmingly that she forgot all about the time, and the clock began to strike twelve when she thought it no more than eleven.

At once she sprang up and ran as nimbly as a deer out of the room, and was going in great haste down the broad staircase that led to the palace entrance when one of her slippers dropped off. She could not wait to pick it up, for the clock had reached its final stroke, and then in a twinkling she was a gay lady no more, but only a shabby kitchen girl hurrying down the steps. The splendid coach and six horses, the driver and footmen had vanished,

and on the ground lay a scooped-out pumpkin, while
six mice, a rat, and two lizards were scurrying away
to find hiding-places.

Cinderella reached home quite out of breath, and
of her grand apparel nothing remained save a little
glass slipper. When the sisters returned from the
ball Cinderella asked them whether they had been
well entertained and whether the beautiful princess
was there.

"Yes," they replied, "we enjoyed the ball very much and the princess was there, but she ran away just as the clock struck twelve, and no one knows who she is any more than they did before."

When Cinderella fled the prince had stood in amazement a moment and then pursued her, but she was too swift for him. However, as he was running down the stairway he noticed the little glass slipper that she had lost and he picked it up. Then he went on and questioned the guards at the palace gates whether they had seen a princess going out. "No," said they, "the only person who has passed out of the gates for over an hour is a poorly dressed girl just gone, and how such a person as she happened to be in the palace, we cannot tell."

The prince, during the days following, caused inquiries to be made everywhere for the princess, and when the search failed he grew ill with disappointment. Then the king, who dearly loved his son, called a council and asked his ministers what they thought ought to be done in order to discover the princess.

"It is my advice," said the chief minister, "that you should cause a proclamation to be made all over the kingdom that the prince will marry her whose foot the slipper he found will just fit."

This plan was adopted, and the slipper was tried on by all the noble ladies of the land — but in vain. Then it was carried from one fine house to another among the gentry, until at last it came to the home of the proud sisters. Each of them did all she possibly could to thrust her foot into the dainty slipper, but the attempt failed. Cinderella, who was present, now laughed and said, "Suppose I were to try."

The sisters ridiculed her. "What an idea!" they said, "to think of its fitting your clumsy foot."

But the gentleman who had brought the slipper looked at Cinderella and said that it was no more than fair she should have the chance she asked, for he had orders to let every young maiden in the kingdom who pleased try on the slipper. So Cinderella sat down while the sisters looked on contemptuously; yet no sooner did she put her little foot to the slipper than it went on at once and fitted like wax. The sisters were amazed, and their astonishment increased tenfold when Cinderella drew the mate to the slipper from her pocket and put it on the other foot.

Just at that moment the fairy appeared, and touching Cinderella's clothes with her wand made them once more the robes of a princess, and then the two sisters recognized her for the beautiful stranger they had seen at the ball.

Now the gentleman in waiting conducted Cinderella away to the palace of the prince. She was received by the prince with great joy, and in a short time they were married, and they lived happily ever after.

HOP-O'-MY-THUMB

THERE was once a wood-cutter and his wife who had seven children, all boys. The eldest was only twelve years old, and the youngest was five, and none of them was large enough to do much toward earning a living, so that their parents had to work very hard to get food and clothing for them. What made matters worse was that the youngest child was sickly and weak, and he was so small that his father and mother called him Hop-o'-my-Thumb. Yet the little, weak boy was gifted with a great deal of sense, and though he never had much to say, he noticed all that went on around him. The year that he was five the harvest failed and the wood-cutter and his wife found it more and more difficult to supply their large family with food. Finally they had spent their last penny and there was only a single loaf of bread left in the house, and when that was eaten they knew they must starve.

That evening, after the children were all in bed, the father and mother sat by the fire thinking sadly of the dismal fate that awaited them. "My dear wife," said the wood-cutter at length, "I have something to propose to you. It is plain that we must perish, but I cannot bear to see our children die of hunger, and I am resolved to lose them to-morrow in the forest. They cannot be worse off than they are at home, and perhaps the fairies will take care of them. We will go very deep into the woods, and while the children are busy tying up fagots we will slip away and leave them."

"No, no," said the wife, "I could never do such a thing."

"But if we don't do that," said the wood-cutter, "they will die here before our eyes, crying with hunger," and he argued until his wife consented to his plan, and then she went weeping to bed.

The parents thought the children were all asleep while they talked. However, Hop-o'-my-Thumb was wide awake and he heard what was said and he never slept any that night for thinking of what he should do. Early in the morning he crept out of bed and ran to a brook near the house and filled his pockets with small white pebbles. Then he went back indoors, and by and by the family ate half of the one loaf of bread and started as usual for their day's work in the forest.

The father led the way and Hop-o'-my-Thumb, who came along behind all the others, dropped the white pebbles one by one from his pockets. The wood-cutter kept on into the very thickest of the woods, and then he began chopping with his ax, and the mother and children picked up the brush and tied it into bundles. They worked thus until toward nightfall, when the parents stole away, and as soon as they were out of their children's sight they hurried back to their home. There they sat silent in the lonely house for a long time, and the sun went down and it was getting dark. Then came a rap at the door, and in walked a man who had been sent by the lord of the manor with a present of ten crowns and a haunch of venison.

"My lord, the baron, is sorry for the distress of his people," said the man, "and he is going to help them, and those who have large families like you are to get the most."

The man then departed to convey assistance to another suffering household. "Oh!" cried the wife, "if only our children were here to eat of this good food. Let us go to the forest and find them."

"No," responded the husband sorrowfully, "it would do no good to seek them now. If the fairies have not taken care of them they must have been eaten by wolves before this time."

Then the mother wept and would not be comforted. " I want my children," she wailed.

But the children had not been eaten by wolves. As soon as they discovered that they were alone, Peter, the oldest boy, began to call, "Father and mother, where are you ? "

No voice answered him, and then he and all the little boys except Hop-o'-my-Thumb ran hither and thither shouting for their parents and crying. Hop-o'-my-Thumb waited until he could make himself heard, and then said, " Fear not, brothers, our father and mother have left us here, but I will lead you safely home."

" And why did they leave us ? " asked Peter.

Hop-o'-my-Thumb told them what he had over-heard and how he had strewed the white pebbles to guide them back. " Just follow me," said he ; "and let us start at once, for it will soon be dark."

So keeping his eyes on the line of pebbles, he hurried along, and the others followed him. They reached home, but because their parents had abandoned them they were afraid they would not be welcome, and instead of going in they huddled under a window at the back of the house to listen. They heard the man come with the money and the venison, and when their mother began to cry they ran around to the front of the house and in at the door, shouting, "Here we are, mother!"

She hugged them every one, and now, instead of crying for sorrow, she cried for gladness. The wood-cutter was rejoiced, too, and he helped start a fire, and soon some slices of venison were broiling before the flames and the family was presently eating the best supper they had had for a long time.

Several weeks passed, and while the venison and the money lasted the wood-cutter got along very well, but the famine grew worse and worse, and the lord of the manor could not send his tenants any more supplies. So at last the wood-cutter thought his family must surely starve, and he and his wife talked the matter over late one night and decided they would take the children again into the forest and lose them.

They talked in whispers, that Hop-o'-my-Thumb might not know what they said even if he chanced to be awake, but he had very keen ears and he heard in spite of their caution. He thought he would get some more pebbles in the morning, but when morning came the parents kept a sharp watch of him and would not let him go out of the house.

He was much troubled by this at first. However, the mother gave them each a slice of dry bread for their breakfast, and Hop-o'-my-Thumb said to himself, " I can use bread crumbs instead of pebbles," and he put his slice of bread into his pocket.

They went deeper than ever into the forest this time, and Hop-o'-my-Thumb followed behind the others and scattered bread crumbs all the way. The day was spent in working, as was their custom, but toward evening the father proposed the children should play a game of hide and seek, and while they were playing he and the mother hurried off and left them.

When the children found that they had been deserted again there was much bitter crying, but Hop-o'-my-Thumb said, " Do not weep, my dear brothers. I will take you home."

They then started to follow the trail of bread crumbs, but the birds had eaten them all up, and the children were very much distressed. " Well," said Hop-o'-my-Thumb after thinking a minute, " we must not waste the twilight in tears. Come along, and we will see if we can find some shelter for the night."

So Hop-o'-my-Thumb led the way. Night came

on, and the wind among the trees seemed to them like the howling of wolves, so that every moment they thought they would be eaten up. They hardly dared speak a word. Presently Hop-o'-my-Thumb climbed to the top of a tall tree to look about for some path out of the forest. He saw no path, but far away was a light shining. "There must be a house where that light is," said he, and though he could not see the light when he returned to the ground, he knew which direction to take.

The little boys hurried along and by and by they came out of the forest, and there stood a great castle. The light Hop-o'-my-Thumb had seen shone through an open door. They went to the door and looked in and saw a woman busy at a fireplace roasting a whole sheep. Hop-o'-my-Thumb rapped to attract her attention.

"What do you want?" said she, turning and looking at them.

"We are poor children who have lost our way in the forest," replied Hop-o'-my-Thumb, "and we beg you for charity's sake to grant us a night's lodging."

"Alas! my little darlings," said the woman, "you do not know where you are come. This is the house of an ogre who would like nothing better

17

than to eat you. I am the cook here and I know
very well what he likes to eat."

"Then what can we do?" said Hop-o'-my-
Thumb; "for if you refuse to give us shelter the
wolves will tear us to pieces in the forest."

"Well, perhaps I can hide you," the old woman
responded; "so you may come in," and as soon
as they entered the room she shut the door.

The children went to the fire and sat down to
warm themselves. Just as they were beginning to
get warm they heard heavy footsteps outside.
"That is the ogre," said the woman in a whisper.
"Make haste and crawl under the bed."

No sooner were they out of sight than the ogre
walked in. "Is my supper ready?" he asked, and
sat down at the table.

The old woman called in another servant and the
two of them lifted the sheep that was roasting
before the fire onto a great platter, and then took
up the platter and placed it before the ogre. The
sheep was half raw, but he liked it that way. When
he had finished he began to sniff right and left.
"I smell fresh meat!" he said.

"It must be the calf I have skinned and hung in
the pantry for your breakfast," explained the old
woman.

Then the ogre looked toward the fireplace and saw a little shoe lying there that one of the boys had taken off. The ogre stamped over to the fireplace and picked up the shoe. "What is this?" he asked in a terrible voice.

"Why, that must be a shoe which belongs to your oldest daughter's doll," said the cook.

At that moment poor Peter, who happened to have a bad cold, sneezed.

"Ah!" exclaimed the ogre shaking his fist at the cook, "you have been deceiving me, and I would eat you if you were not so old and tough."

Then he dragged the children from under the bed and never paid the least heed to their appeals for mercy. He would have eaten one or two of them that night, but the old woman said, "See how lean they are. They have been half starved. They will be much fatter if we feed them for a few days."

The ogre took up Hop-o'-my-Thumb and pinched his arms. "You are right," said he; "this child is nothing but bones."

Then the woman gave the boys a good supper and put them to bed, and they were so tired that they fell asleep at once and did not wake till morning. Hop-o'-my-Thumb was on the watch all that day for some chance to escape, but the ogre had seven daughters and he ordered them to keep the boys from straying. The daughters had small gray eyes and large mouths and long sharp teeth. They were young and not very vicious as yet; but they showed what they would be, for they had already begun to bite little boys, and their captives did not in the least enjoy their company.

When night came and all the family had gone to bed, Hop-o'-my-Thumb lay awake until every one else was asleep, and then he roused his brothers and whispered, " Come, we must be off."

They all dressed quickly and quietly and followed him, and he led the way downstairs and out a back door into the garden, and by climbing up some vines that grew on the wall they got outside. They did not dare go far for fear of wolves, and they crept into a heap of straw that lay beside the wall and waited for daylight. Hop-o'-my-Thumb thought he could find the way home by keeping along the edge of the forest, and as soon as there was light enough for them to see they started.

The ogre was not an early riser and he did not think of the boys until after he had eaten breakfast. He was very angry when they were not to be found. " Quick ! " he shouted to his cook,

The ogre in his seven-league boots hunts for Hop-O'-My-Thumb and his brothers

"get me my seven-league boots, that I may go and catch them."

With those magic boots he could go a great distance at a single step, and he would have caught the little boys at once if he had known just where to look for them. As it was, he hunted in every direction. He strode from hill to hill and stepped over wide rivers as easily as if they had been brooks. Late in the afternoon the boys had arrived within about a mile of home, and they were hurrying along a hillside when they saw the ogre coming in their direction. Luckily he had not seen them and they scurried into a cave that chanced to be close by.

The ogre had done so much racing about that he was tired, and when he came to the hillside where the boys were he lay down over the very cave in which they had taken refuge, and there he went to sleep and snored with a sound like thunder that frightened the little boys very much. "Now," said Hop-o'-my-Thumb to his brothers, "the rest of you run away home. I'm going to see if I can get those boots."

When they had gone he crept up to where the ogre lay and gently pulled off his boots and got into them himself. The boots as worn by the ogre

were very large and heavy, but they were magic
boots that fitted themselves to whatever feet were

put into them, and so they were just right for
Hop-o'-my-Thumb.

The ogre had been partly awakened when his
boots were pulled off, and Hop-o'-my-Thumb
scarcely had time to get them on his own feet
before the giant suddenly opened his eyes and sat
up. He saw what had happened and he roared
with anger. Off went Hop-o'-my-Thumb and
the ogre jumped to his feet and gave chase. But
he was no match for the speed of the little lad
with the seven-league boots. Not far from where
the giant had lain down was a precipice, and
Hop-o'-my-Thumb stepped off this cliff to a hilltop opposite. The ogre, who was rushing after
him, forgot that he did not have the boots on and
must be cautious, and he fell from the cliff with

a crash that made the rocks echo far and near, and that was the end of him.

While Hop-o' my-Thumb had been at the ogre's house he had found out where the ogre kept his money, and there was a little window to the treasure-room too small for any ordinary person to get through, but which would admit Hop-o'-my-Thumb easily. "Unless I can get some of that money to buy food with," said he, "my father and mother and all the rest of us will starve;" and he decided he would go and see what he could do.

His boots took him to the ogre's house in a twinkling, and he slipped in at the little window of the treasure-room and loaded himself down with all the gold he could carry. Then he went home, and his father and mother were very happy to have their children all back, and with the money Hop-o'-my-Thumb brought they got all the food they needed and passed through the famine quite comfortably.

BEAUTY AND THE BEAST

THERE was once a wealthy merchant who had six children, three sons and three daughters ; and he loved his children more than he loved his riches and was always trying to make them happy. The three daughters were very handsome, but the youngest was the most attractive of all. While she was little she was called Beauty, and when she grew up she still kept the same name — and she was as good as she was beautiful. She spent much of her time studying, and when not engaged with her books she was busy doing all she could to make her home pleasant for her father. The older sisters were not like Beauty. They were proud of their riches and cared little for study, and they were constantly driving in the parks or attending balls, operas, and plays.

Thus things went along until misfortunes began to overtake the merchant in his business, and one evening he came home and told his family that storms at sea had destroyed his ships, and fire had burned his warehouses. " My riches are gone," said he, " and I have nothing I can call my own but a little farm far off in the country. To that little farm we must all go, now, and earn our daily living with our hands."

The daughters wept at the idea of leading such a different life, and the older ones said they would not go, for they had plenty of friends who would invite them to stay in the town. But they were mistaken. Their friends, who were numerous when the family was rich, now kept away and said one to the other, " We are sorry for the merchant and his family, of course. However, we have cares of our own, and we could n't be expected to help them ; and, really, if those two older girls are having their pride humbled it is no more than they deserve. Let them go and give themselves quality airs milking the cows and minding their dairy and see how they like it."

So the family went to live on the little farm in the country, and the merchant and his sons ploughed and sowed the fields, and Beauty rose at four o'clock every morning to get breakfast for them. After the breakfast things were out of the way she busied herself about the other housework, and when there was nothing else to do she would sit at her spinning-wheel, singing as she spun, or perhaps would take a little time for reading. The work was hard at first, yet when she became used to it she enjoyed it, and her eyes were brighter and her cheeks more rosy than ever before.

Her two sisters did not change their habits so easily, and they were wretched. They were always thinking of the wealth they had lost, and they did not get up till ten o'clock and did very little work after they were up, but spent most of the time sauntering about and complaining.

A year passed and then the merchant received news that one of his ships which he had believed to be lost had come safely into port with a rich cargo. This news nearly turned the heads of the two eldest daughters, who thought that now they could soon leave the little farm and return to the gay city. As soon as their father made ready to go to the port to attend to the unlading and sale of the ship's cargo they begged him to buy them new gowns and hats and all manner of trinkets.

Then the merchant said, " And what shall I bring you, Beauty ? "

" The only thing I wish for is to see you come home safely," she answered.

Her father was pleased, but he thought she ought to tell him of something he might bring her from the town. " Well, dear father," said she,

" as you insist, I would like to have you bring
me a rose, for I have not seen one since we
came here."

The good man now set out on his journey, but
when he reached the port he found that a former
partner had taken charge of the ship's goods and
disposed of them. The man would not turn over
the money he had received to the merchant, and
the merchant was obliged to sue for it in the
courts. But what he recovered barely paid the
costs, and at the end of six months of trouble and
expense he started for his little farm as poor as
when he came.

He travelled day after day until he was within
thirty miles of home, and he was thinking of the
pleasure he would have in seeing his children again
when he lost his way in a great forest through which
he had to pass. Night came on cold and rainy,
and the poor man grew faint with hunger. But
presently he saw bright lights some way off shining
through the trees, and he turned his horse toward
them and soon came into a long avenue of great
oaks. This led to a splendid palace that was lit
from top to bottom. Yet when the merchant
entered the courtyard no one met him, and when
he halooed he received no answer. His horse kept

on toward an open stable door, and he dismounted and led the creature inside and hitched it to a manger that was full of hay and oats.

The merchant now sought the castle and went into a large hall where he found a good fire, and a table ple fully set with food, but not a soul did he see. While he stood by the fire drying himself he said, " How fortunate I am to find such shelter, for I should have perished this stormy night out in the forest. But I can't imagine where the people of this house can be, and I hope its master will excuse the liberty I have taken."

He waited for some time and the clock struck eleven. No one came, and then, weak for want of food, he sat down at the table and ate heartily; yet all the while he was fearful that he was trespassing and might be severely dealt with for his presumption. After he had finished eating he felt less timid and he concluded he would look for a chamber. So he left the hall and passed through several splendid rooms till he came to one in which was a comfortable bed, and there he spent the night.

On awaking the following morning he was surprised to find a new suit of clothes laid out for him , on a chair by the bedside, marked with his name, and with ten gold pieces in every pocket. His own clothes, which were much the worse for wear and had been wet through by the storm, had disappeared. "Surely," said he, "this palace belongs to some kind fairy who has seen and pitied my distresses."

In the hall where he had supped the night before he found the table prepared for his breakfast, and after he had eaten he went out into a great garden full of beautiful flowers and shrubbery. As he walked along he passed under a bower of roses. "Ah," said he stopping, "I had no money when I left the town to buy the gifts my older daughters wanted, and my mind has been so full of my troubles that I have not thought of the rose for which Beauty asked, until this moment. She shall have one of these," and he reached up and plucked one.

No sooner had he done this than a great beast came suddenly forth from a side path where he had been hidden by a hedge and stood before the merchant. "This place is mine," said the beast in his deep, gruff voice. "Why do you pick my flowers?"

"Forgive me, my lord," begged the merchant, throwing himself on his knees before the beast. "I did not know I was giving offence. I only wanted to carry a rose to one of my daughters."

"You have daughters, have you?" said the beast.

" Now, listen !   This palace is lonely and I want
one of your daughters to come here and live."

"Oh, sir !" cried the merchant, "do not ask
that."

"Nothing else will appease me," the beast responded.   " I promise no harm will be done her.
So take the rose you have picked and go at once and

tell your daughters what I have said; and in case
not one of them will come you must return yourself
and be prisoned for the rest of your days in the
palace dungeon."

" My lord," replied the merchant, " I shall not
let a child of mine suffer for me, and you may as
well lock me up in your dungeon now as later."

" No," the beast said, " you go home and consult
with your daughters first."

" I am in your power," said the merchant, " and
I can only obey you."

Then he went to the stable and mounted his
horse and by night he reached home.   His children
ran out to greet him, but instead of receiving their
caresses with pleasure the tears rolled down his
cheeks, and he handed the rose to Beauty, saying,
" Little do you think how dear that will cost your
poor father; " and he related all the sad adventures
that had befallen him.   " To-morrow," said the
merchant in closing, " I shall return to the beast."

" I can't let you do that, dear father," said Beauty.
" I am going in your stead."

" Not so, sister," cried her three brothers, " we
will seek out the monster and either kill him or die
ourselves."

" You could accomplish nothing," declared the

merchant, " for he lives in an enchanted palace and has invisible helpers with whom you could not hope to contend successfully."

" How unfortunate it all is ! " said the older girls. " What a pity, Beauty, that you did not do as we did and ask for something sensible."

" Well," said Beauty, " who could have guessed that to ask for a rose would cause so much misery ? However, the fault is plainly mine, and I shall have to suffer the consequences."

Her father tried to dissuade her from her purpose, but she insisted, and the next morning he mounted his horse and, with Beauty sitting behind him, he started for the beast's palace. They arrived late in the afternoon and rode down the long avenue of oaks and into the silent courtyard to the door of the stable where the horse had been kept before. Then they dismounted, and after the merchant had led the horse into the stable and seen it comfortably housed for the night they went into the palace.

A cheerful fire was blazing in the big hall and the table was daintily spread with most delicious food. They sat down to this repast, but were too sad to eat much and were soon through. Just then the beast came in and addressed the merchant. " Honest man," said he, " I am glad that you could be trusted.

I was rude and thre.. ....g toward you yesterday, but it seemed necess-ary. However, in the end, I think you will have nothing :o regret. Spend the night here and to-morrow go your way."

"This is my daughter, Beauty," said the merchant

The beast bowed and said, "My lady, I am ve.y grateful to you for coming, and I beg you to remember that I am not what you think me. But I cannot tell you what I really am, for I am under a spell. This spell I hore you will be able to remove."

So saying, th·   : withdrew and left the merchant and his c. ghter sitting by the fire. "What the beast m.. .s," said the merchant, "I do not know; but he talks very courteously."

Then they sat long in silence, but at last arose; and they each hunted up a chamber and retired to try to sleep.

On the morrow they found breakfast prepared for them in the hall, and after they had eaten, the merchant bade his daughter an affectionate farewell. He went to the stable for his horse. It was all ready for him to mount, and to his surprise the saddlebags were full of gold. "Ah, well!" said he, "here is wealth once more, but it cannot make up for the loss of my dear daughter."

Beauty watched him ride away. As soon as he was gone she threw herself down on a cushioned window-seat and cried till she fell asleep; and while she slept she dreamed she was walking by a brook bordered with trees and lamenting her sad fate, when a young prince, handsomer than any man she had ever seen, came to her and said, " Ah, Beauty, you are not so unfortunate as you suppose. You will have your reward."

She awoke late in the day a good deal refreshed and comforted, and after a little she decided she would walk about and see something of the palace in which she was to live. She found much to admire and presently came to a door on which was written BEAUTY'S ROOM.

She opened the door and entered a splendidly furnished apartment where were a multitude of books and pictures, a harpsichord and many comfortable chairs and couches. She picked up a book that lay on a table, and on the fly-leaf she found written in golden letters these words:

" Your wishes and commands shall be obeyed. You are here the queen over everything."

" Alas! " she thought, " my chief wish just at this moment is to see what my poor father is about."

While she was thinking this she perceived some
movement in a mirror on the wall in front of her,

and when she looked into the mirror she saw her
father arriving home and her sisters and brothers
meeting him. The vision faded quickly away, but
Beauty felt very thankful she had been allowed such
a pleasure. "This beast shows a great deal of kindness," said she, glancing about the attractive room.
"He must be a far better creature than we have
imagined."

She did not see the beast until evening, and then
he came and asked if he might sup with her, and

she replied that he could. But she would much rather have eaten alone, for she could not help trembling in his presence. As long as they sat at the table soft, beautiful music was played, though whence it came or who were the musicians she could not discover. The beast talked to Beauty with great politeness and intelligence, yet his gruff voice startled her every time he spoke. When they had nearly finished he said, " I suppose you think my appearance extremely ugly."

"Yes," said Beauty, "for I cannot tell a lie, but I think you are very good."

" You show a most gracious spirit," said the beast, " in not judging me wholly by my uncouth exterior. I will do anything I can to make you happy here."

" You are very kind, Beast," she replied. " Indeed, when I think of your good heart, you no longer seem to me so ugly."

As they rose from the supper table, the beast said, " Beauty, do you think you could ever care enough for me to kiss me ? "

She faltered out, " No, Beast," and he turned and left the room sighing so deeply that she pitied him.

In the days and weeks which followed Beauty saw no one save the beast, yet there were invisible servants who did everything possible for her comfort and pleasure. She and the beast always had supper together, and his conversation never failed to be entertaining and agreeable. By degrees she grew accustomed to his shaggy ugliness and learned to mind it less and to think more of his many amiable qualities. The only thing that pained her was that when he was about to leave her at the end of supper he was sure to ask if she thought she could sometime care enough for him to kiss him.

Three months passed, and one day Beauty looked in her mirror and saw a double wedding at her father's cottage. Her sisters were being married to two gentlemen of the region. Not long afterward her mirror showed her that her three brothers had enlisted for soldiers and her father was left alone. A few days more elapsed and she saw that her father was sick. The sight made her weep, and in the evening she told the beast what her mirror had revealed to her and that she wished to go and nurse her father.

"And will you return at the end of a week if you go?" asked the beast.

"Yes," she replied.

"I cannot refuse anything you ask," said he. "I will have a swift horse ready for you at sunrise to-morrow."

The next day at sunrise Beauty found the swift horse saddled for her in the courtyard, and away she went like the wind through the forest toward her father's cottage. When she arrived, the old merchant was so overjoyed at seeing her that his sickness quickly left him and the two spent a most happy week together.

As soon.as the seven days were past she returned to the castle of the beast, which she reached late in the afternoon. Supper time came and the food was served as usual, but the beast was absent and Beauty was a good deal alarmed. " Oh, I hope nothing has happened to him," she said. " He was so good and considerate."

After waiting a short time she went to look for the beast. She ran hastily through all the apartments of the palace, but the beast was not there ; and then in the twilight she hurried out to the garden, and by the borders of a fountain she found the beast lying as if dead.

" Dear, dear Beast," she cried, dropping on her knees beside him, " what has happened? " and she leaned over and kissed his hairy cheek.

. At once a change came over the beast, and on the grass beside the fountain lay a handsome prince. He opened his eyes and said feebly, " My lady, I thank you. A wicked magician had condemned me to assume the form of an ugly beast until some beautiful maiden consented to kiss me. But I think you are the only maiden in the world kind-hearted enough to have had affection for me in the ugly form the magician had given me. When you went away to your father I was so lonely I could no longer eat or amuse myself, and I became so weak that to-day, when I was walking here in the garden, I fell and could not rise."

Then Beauty filled a cup with water from the fountain and lifted him up so that he could drink. That revived him somewhat and with her help he rose to his feet. The enchantment had been removed from the palace as well as from the prince, and the servants were no longer invisible.

"Call for help," said the prince; and when she called, several men instantly came to their aid and carried the prince to the palace. Once there, warmth, food, and happiness went far toward restoring him. The next morning he sent for Beauty's father to come and make his home with them, and not long afterward Beauty and the prince were married and they lived with great joy and contentment in their palace ever after.

THE FATE OF A LITTLE OLD WOMAN

LAST Monday morning at six o'clock in the evening, as I was sailing over the tops of the mountains in my little boat, I met two men on horseback riding on a donkey; and I asked them could they tell me whether the little old woman was dead yet who was hanged a week ago Friday for drowning herself in a shower of feathers.

"No," said they, "we cannot inform you; but if you will go to the next town beyond the mountains and call on Sir Gammer Vans he can tell you all about it."

"But how am I to know his house?" I asked.

"Ho! 'tis easy enough," they replied, "for 'tis a wooden house built of brick, standing alone by itself in the midst of sixty or seventy other houses just like it."

"Then nothing in the world can be easier," said I, and I went on my way.

This Sir Gammer Vans was a giant, and when I got to his house he popped out of a little thumb-bottle from behind the door.

" How d' ye do ? " says he.

" Very well, I thank you," says I.

" Have some supper with me this morning," says he.

" Certainly," says I.

So he gave me a slice of coffee and a cup of cold beef; and there was a big dog under the table who picked up all the crumbs.

When we had finished drinking the beef and eating the coffee, I said, " Sir Gammer, do you happen to know whether the little old woman is —— "

But I said no more, for at that moment we heard a distant shouting and Sir Gammer Vans interrupted me by saying, " I wonder if that can be my bird-hunter who catches fish for me?"

" Why not go to the door and look out of the window and see?" I asked.

" So I would," said he, " but I have the gout in my left foot a trifle above my right knee which makes it painful for me to move about. Pray, go in my stead and tell me if you can see any one just out of sight beyond the woods that grow in the bare field where my wheat is ripening for the harvest."

I looked as he requested. " Yes," I replied, " I see a man running in this direction as fast as he can walk."

" Ah," said Sir Gammer Vans, " he is no doubt bringing me a fish."

Soon the man arrived and was admitted to the house. At once he took a fine salmon from an empty basket he carried, and said, " I shot that salmon with my club as it was flying over a barn in the valley on the next hilltop."

"Very good !" says Sir Gammer, "and now you may get it ready for us to eat for breakfast this evening."

So the man put the fish in a pot of water turned bottom upwards on the fire, and when it had boiled for three hours he took the salmon out hard frozen and made it into the best apple-pie I ever tasted.

We ate the pie all up that evening for breakfast. Then I rode away in my little boat over the mountain tops, and Sir Gammer Vans had not told me whether or not the little old woman was dead who had been hanged for drowning herself in a shower of feathers ; for I had forgotten to ask him.

THE DONKEY, THE TABLE,
AND THE STICK

THERE was once a poor tailor who had a son named Jack; and they two were all there was to the family, unless we count the goat that gave them the milk they had to drink. They took very good care of the goat and Jack led her every day down to the riverside where the grass grew greenest, that she might have plenty to eat. In the evening Jack would go down by the river to fetch the goat home. "Well, goat," he would say, "have you had enough?" And the goat would reply,

"I am so full
I cannot pull
Another blade of grass — ba! baa!"

"Then come along," Jack would say, and he would tie a cord to the goat's neck and lead her home to her stall and fasten her up.

Afterward he would tell his father that he had brought the goat home, and his father would ask, "Has the goat had plenty to eat to-day?"

"Oh, yes!" Jack would answer, "she is so full she no more can pull."

But one evening the tailor was looking at the goat and he thought she seemed rather thin, and he said, "My dear goat, are you full?"

And the goat replied,

> "How can I be full?
> There was nothing to pull,
> Though I looked all about me — ba! baa!"

"What is this I hear?" cried the tailor, angrily, for he had a hasty temper. "My son has been deceiving me then."

He went to the house and found Jack. "You said the goat was full!" he shouted, "and she has been hungry all the time."

The tailor was so enraged that Jack was afraid he was going to beat him, and the lad hurried out of the house and down the road as fast as he could go. "The farther I get the better," said he, "for it will be a good while before I shall dare show my face at home again."

So the next day there was no Jack to take the goat to the feeding-place by the waterside, and the tailor had to lead her there himself. The food was plentiful and he said to her, " Now for once you can eat to your heart's content."

Then he went back to his work, and in the evening he came to get the goat, and he said to her, " Well, goat, are you full ? "

And the goat answered,

> " I am so full
> I could not pull
> Another blade of grass — ba ! baa !"

" Come home then," said the tailor, and he led her to her stall and fastened her up. " You are full this time," he said as he was leaving her; but the goat said,

> " How can I be full ?
> There was nothing to pull,
> Though I looked all about me — ba ! baa ! "

When the tailor heard that he knew the goat was not speaking the truth. " If she lies to-day," said he, " no doubt she lied yesterday, and I have made a mistake in not believing my son."

Then he laid hold of the goat and exclaimed, "Wait a minute, you ungrateful beast! I will give you a beating that you will long remember!"

He picked up a stout stick, dragged the goat from her stall and belabored her very heartily until she broke away from him and ran off. Week after week passed, and the tailor felt very sad. He was all alone and there was not a day that he did not wish his son would return home, but no one knew where Jack had gone.

Now what had happened to Jack was this — he ran and he ran until he ran right up against a little old woman who was walking along the road. "Whither so fast, my lad?" she asked.

"I beg your pardon," replied Jack. "I have left home to go out in the wide world and seek my fortune, and I was in a hurry."

"Why not apprentice yourself to my husband then?" said the old woman. "He is a miller and he needs a helper, and I can promise you that he will pay good wages."

Jack promptly agreed to accept the work offered, for he was very hungry and tired. So the old woman took Jack to the mill, and he served the miller for a year and a day. Then the miller told Jack he would pay him his wages. "You have behaved very well," said he, "and I am going to give you a donkey, but this donkey will draw no cart and carry no sack."

"What is the good of him then?" asked Jack.

"He spits out gold and silver," replied the miller. "You have but to pull one of his ears and he will begin at once to 'He-haw! he-haw!' and when he brays there will drop from his mouth silver six-pences and half-crowns and golden guineas."

"Very good," said the lad, and he thanked the miller and set forth, leading the donkey behind him. "I shall have no cares, now," said Jack. "My purse will be always full, and wherever I go I shall live on the best."

By and by he stopped at an inn, and the landlord was for taking the donkey from him to tie him up, but Jack said, "Oh, no, you need not trouble to do that. I will go to the stable with him myself, and then I shall know where to find him."

So the young apprentice took his donkey to the stable and afterward went into the inn and ordered as good a supper as the landlord could provide. The innkeeper stared, for he did not think that a man who took care of his own donkey could have much to spend, and he refused to serve him without being paid beforehand. "You need not

worry," said Jack, " I can get plenty of money,"
and he went off to the stable, pulled one of the
donkey's ears and got a pocket full of gold and
silver.

The landlord wondered what Jack meant by
saying he could get plenty of money. " I will

follow the lad and see where he keeps his wealth,"
he said.

So the landlord slipped after Jack and saw
everything he did through a crack in the stable
door. " Dear me ! " said he, " that is an easy way
of getting ducats. A purse of money such as
that donkey seems to be is no bad thing."

After Jack had eaten supper and gone to bed the
landlord visited the stable again, and this time he

led the gold donkey away and tied another in his place.

The next morning, early, the apprentice went to the stable and got the donkey, never doubting that he had the right one. " I will go back to my father, now," said he. " His anger must have cooled long ago, and when he knows I have this gold donkey he will receive me kindly."

By noon he came to his father's house, and his father was rejoiced to see him. " What trade have you taken up, my son?" said he, after the first greetings were over with.

" I am a miller, dear father," answered Jack.

" And what have you brought home with you to show for your year's work?" asked the father.

" I have brought home a donkey," said Jack, " that furnishes me with more money than I know what to do with. Why, with that donkey I can make you rich with no trouble at all! "

" That is very fine," said the tailor. " I am getting old, and it is irksome work snipping and sewing so unceasingly. I have long wanted to quit it. ·I suppose now I need not labor with my needle any more."

" No," replied Jack, " throw your needle away and call in the neighbors. I will make them rich, too."

So the tailor rushed out and went from house to house telling all the people of the village the good news. Soon they came flocking back with him and then Jack made them a speech as they stood roundabout the house, and after that he led his donkey into the midst of the crowd and began pulling the beast's ears. But, though Jack pulled and pulled and the donkey he-hawed and he-hawed, no silver or gold was forthcoming. The crowd laughed, and the tailor was so angry at Jack that the young man thought his father was going to thrash him and he took to his heels. He ran and ran till he came bang against a door and burst it open, and there he was in a carpenter's shop.

"You seem to be in great haste," said the carpenter.

"Yes," replied Jack, "but I will go no farther if you will give me work."

"All right," the carpenter responded, "be my apprentice and I will pay you well."

Jack agreed, and he served the carpenter for a year and a day. Then the master said, "I will now give you your wages. I will let you have ten shillings in money, which will very likely come handy, and you may take this little table. When you are hungry you have only to say, 'Table, be covered,' and at once it will have a clean cloth on it and dishes and lots to eat and drink."

The young apprentice thought he was set up for life, and he put the ten shillings in his pocket and took the table on his back and went merrily on his way. At length he came to the inn where he had stopped the year before. It was full of guests, but they bade Jack welcome, and asked him to sit down with them to eat, as otherwise he might not be able to get anything.

"You are very kind," said Jack, "yet I am not so badly off as you think, and instead of accepting your invitation I will ask you all to share with me a feast of my own providing."

Then they laughed, for they thought he was joking; but he brought in his little wooden table and said, "Table, be covered!"

Without delay the table was set with much better food than the landlord had been able to give his guests, and the odor of it greeted their noses very agreeably. "Fall to, my good friends," said Jack, and the guests, when they understood how things were, needed no second asking.

They went at the food most valiantly, and as often as a dish was emptied a full one took its place. All the while the landlord stood in a corner watching proceedings with keen interest. " Such cooking as that would make my inn prosper," said he to himself.

When at last the party broke up, Jack left his wishing-table standing against the wall and went to bed. The landlord locked up and went to bed also, but he could not sleep for thinking of Jack's table. He remembered that he had in his attic an old table very like it, and finally he got up and fetched that table down and exchanged it for Jack's. Jack, none the wiser, rose the next day early, paid his reckoning, took the worthless table on his back and set off to see his father. He never once stopped by the way, not even for breakfast, and by nine o'clock he reached his father's house. The tailor was rejoiced to see his son, and asked him what he had been doing all the long year that he had been gone.

" Oh," said Jack, " I have learned to be a carpenter."

" That is a good trade," said the tailor, " and what have you brought back with you ? "

" I have brought this little table," Jack responded.

The tailor looked at it on all sides. " Rather a rubbishing old table, I call it," said he.

" But it is a very wonderful one," explained Jack. " I can ask that table for anything I please in the line of food and drink and it furnishes what I call for in no time. Let us invite the neighbors to come and we will all feast and enjoy ourselves."

So the tailor hastened to get the neighbors together, and then Jack put his table in their midst and said, " Table, be covered ! "

But nothing came of his command, and the table remained just as empty as any other table that does not understand talking. Jack felt very foolish then, and the company joked him freely and his father began to upbraid him and grew more and more wrathful, and the young man was frightened and had · no doubt his father was about to chastise him with his cane. So he got away as fast as his legs would carry him, and he ran and ran until he tumbled into a river. A man who happened to be near by pulled him out and said, " I suppose you are not looking for work or you would not be going so fast."

" No," said Jack, " I was not looking for anything, but I want work, nevertheless."

" Well," said the man, " I have a turning shop here on the river bank, and I will take you for an apprentice and pay you well."

So Jack worked for the turner a year and a day, and then his master, to reward him for his labor and his good conduct, handed him a few shillings in money, and after that gave him a sack and told him there was a stick inside of it.

"The sack may be of use to me," said Jack, "but what is the good of the stick?"

"I will tell you," said the master. "If any man does you harm, and you say, 'Out stick, and bang him!' the stick will jump out and will drub him soundly and will not stop until you say, 'Stick, into the sack!'"

The apprentice thanked his master and started on his travels and he was not long in seeking the inn where he had formerly fared so badly. He ate supper, and as he was sitting by the inn-room fire afterward the landlord asked, "What is it you have in that sack which you take such care of?"

"Well," replied Jack, "I don't propose to tell you, but I'll say this — I wouldn't exchange what I have in that bag for a thousand guineas."

That roused the landlord's curiosity more than ever. "What in the world can it be?" thought he. "Perhaps he has a lot of precious stones in his sack."

By and by Jack nodded off into a nap, and as no one else was present the landlord laid hold of the sack and was taking it away when Jack awoke. "Out stick, and bang him!" he cried.

At once the stick flew from the bag and battered the innkeeper on the back, rapped his head and bruised his arms and legs until he fell groaning to the floor.

" Have mercy ! have mercy!" begged the landlord.

" I will have mercy when you give me my table and donkey," said Jack.

" You can have anything you want," said the wretched man, " if only you will make this terrible goblin stick stop beating me."

" Very well," was Jack's response; and then he said, " Stick, into the sack ! "

At once the stick left the man in peace and disappeared into the bag, and the landlord told Jack where he kept the table and the donkey, and promised he should have them whenever he chose to take them. Then he crept off to bed very lame and sore.

The next morning the landlord turned over to Jack the gold donkey and the wishing table, and the young man set out for his father's house. He arrived an hour before noon and the tailor was very glad to see him again and asked what he had learned while he had been away.

" My dear father," answered Jack, " I have been apprenticed to a turner."

"A very ingenious handicraft," said the father, "and what have you brought back with you?"

"A stick in a sack," Jack replied.

"What!" cried the old tailor, "a stick in a sack! Have you gone crazy?"

"But it is not a common stick," Jack explained. "When any man means harm to me I simply say, 'Out stick, and bang him!' and the stick jumps from the sack and gives the fellow such a pounding that he is soon glad to beg my pardon. You remember last year I told you about a wishing table that supplied me with food, and the year before I told you about a donkey that furnished me with money. Well, the table and donkey were stolen from me by a wicked innkeeper, but with this stick I have recovered them both. Now let the neighbors all be sent for and they shall have the finest feast they have ever had in their lives and I will fill their pockets with gold."

So the old tailor called the neighbors together and the son took his little table and said, "Table, be covered!" and at once it was set with a feast that kept the company jolly for a long time.

After that Jack brought the donkey and pulled his ears and the money jingled out of his mouth until they all had as much as they could carry away; and I cannot help thinking it is a great pity that you and I were not there.

The next day the tailor took his needles and thread, his yard measure and his goose and locked them up in a cupboard, and he lived ever after with his son in great ease and luxury.

But what became of the goat, the unlucky cause of Jack's being driven from home? I will tell you. She ran to the woods and into a fox's hole and hid herself. When the fox came home he caught sight of two great eyes staring at him out of the darkness, and the fox was so frightened that he scampered away as fast as he could go until he met a bear.

"Hold on, Brother Fox!" called the bear, "what is the trouble that you should be racing off like that?"

"Oh, dear!" answered the fox, "a grisly beast is sitting in my hole, and he stared at me with fiery eyes."

"I will soon drive him out," said the bear.

So he went to the fox's hole and looked in; but when he caught sight of the goat's gleaming eyes he too was terrified and fled in great haste until he met a bee.

"Stop, Brother Bear, stop!" called the bee. "What has happened? I never knew you to get over the ground so fast before, and you have a very depressed countenance. What has become of your high spirit?"

"You may well ask," the bear replied. "In the fox's hole there sits a grisly beast with fiery eyes and neither the fox nor I can drive him out."

"I am a poor feeble little creature," said the bee, "and I know you despise me, Bear, but I think I can help you."

So the bee flew into the fox's hole and stung the

goat on the head. Then the goat jumped and cried "Baa! Baa!" and ran out like mad into the world; and whither she went no one knows to this hour.

MR. VINEGAR

MR. and Mrs. Vinegar were very poor, and they lived in a shabby little house that they had built with their own hands. It was made of old boards and other rubbish which they had picked up, and it rattled and shook in every high wind. One morning, Mrs. Vinegar, who was a very good housewife, was busily sweeping her kitchen floor when an unlucky thump of the broom against the walls brought down the whole house, clitter-clatter about her ears. Mr. Vinegar had gone to a neighboring thicket to gather some fagots, and she hurried off with much weeping and wailing to tell him of the disaster. When she found him she exclaimed, " Oh, Mr. Vinegar ! Mr. Vinegar ! we are ruined, we are ruined ! I have knocked the house down and it is all to pieces ! "

" My dear," said Mr. Vinegar, " pray do not weep any more. I will go back with you and see what can be done."

So they returned, and Mr. Vinegar said, "Yes, wife, the house is all in bits and we can never live in it again; but here is the door. I will take that on my back and we will go forth to seek our fortune."

With his wife's help he got the door on his back, and off they started. They walked all that day, and by nightfall they were both very tired. They had now come to a thick forest and Mr. Vinegar said, "My love, I will climb up into a tree with this door and you shall follow after."

So he climbed up among the branches of a great tree, and when he had adjusted the door at a level Mrs. Vinegar climbed up also, and they stretched

their weary limbs on it and were soon fast asleep.
But in the middle of the night Mr. Vinegar was
awakened by the sound of voices directly below him.
He looked down and, to his dismay, saw that a
party of robbers were met under the tree to divide
some money they had stolen. "Jack," said one,
"here's five pounds for you; and Bill, here's ten
pounds for you; and Bob, here's three pounds for
you."

Mr. Vinegar was so frightened he could listen no
longer, and he trembled so violently that he shook
the door off the branches on which it lay, and he and
Mrs. Vinegar had to cling to the tree to save themselves from a bad tumble. When the door began to
drop the noise it made startled the robbers and they
looked up to learn the cause, but no sooner did they
do this than the door came down on their heads and
they all ran away greatly terrified.

Mr. and Mrs. Vinegar, however, dared not quit
their tree till broad daylight. Then Mr. Vinegar
scrambled down. "I hope the door was not broken
by its fall," said he as he lifted it.

Just then he espied a number of golden guineas
that had been beneath the door where they had
been dropped on the ground by the robbers in their
haste to get away. "Come down, Mrs. Vinegar!"

20

he cried, "come down, I say! Our fortune is made! Come down, I say!"

Mrs. Vinegar came down as quickly as she could and saw the money with great delight, and when they counted it they found they were the possessors of forty guineas. "Now, my dear," said she, "I'll tell you what you shall do. You must take these forty guineas and go to the nearest town and buy a cow. I can make butter and cheese which you shall sell at market, and we shall then be able to live very comfortably."

"I will do as you say," replied Mr. Vinegar, "and you can stay here till I return."

So he took the money and went off to the nearest town; and there was a fair in the town, and crowds of people. When he arrived he walked about until he saw a beautiful red cow that he thought would just suit him. "Oh, if I only had that cow," said Mr. Vinegar, "I should be the happiest man alive."

Then he offered the forty guineas for the cow and the owner was quite ready to part with it at that price, and the bargain was made. Mr. Vinegar was proud of his purchase, and he led the cow backwards and forwards to show it. But by and by he saw a man playing some bag-pipes — tweedledum, tweedle-dee. The children followed after the bagpipe man, and he appeared to be pocketing a great deal of money.

"What a pleasant and profitable life that musician must lead," said Mr. Vinegar. "If I had that instrument I should be the happiest man alive, and I could earn far more than with this cow."

So he went up to the man and said, "Friend, what a charming instrument that is, and what a deal of money you must make!"

"Why, yes," said the man; "I make a great deal of money, to be sure, and it is a wonderful instrument."

"Oh!" cried Mr. Vinegar, "how I should like to possess it!"

"Well," said the man, "I will exchange it for your red cow."

"Done!" said the delighted Mr. Vinegar.

So the beautiful red cow was given for the bagpipes. Mr. Vinegar walked up and down with his purchase, but in vain he attempted to play a tune, and the children, instead of giving him pennies, hooted and laughed at him. The day was chilly and poor Mr. Vinegar's fingers grew very cold. At last, heartily ashamed and mortified, he was leaving the town when he met a man wearing a fine, thick pair of gloves.

"Oh, my fingers are so very cold!" said Mr. Vinegar to himself. "If I had those warm gloves I should be the happiest man alive."

Then he went up to the man and said to him, "Friend, you seem to have a capital pair of gloves there."

"Yes, truly," replied the man, "these are excellent gloves."

"Well," said Mr. Vinegar, "I should like to have them. I will give you these bagpipes for them."

"All right," said the man, and he took the bagpipes and Mr. Vinegar put on the gloves and felt entirely contented as he trudged along toward the forest.

But the farther he walked the more tired he became, until presently he saw a man coming toward him with a good stout cane in his hand. "Oh!" said Mr. Vinegar, "if I had that cane I should be the happiest man alive."

Then he said to the man, "Friend, what a rare good cane you have."

"Yes," the man responded, "I have used it for many a mile and it has been a great help."

"How would it suit you to give it to me in exchange for these gloves?" asked Mr. Vinegar.

"I will do so willingly," replied the man.

"My hands had become perfectly warm," said Mr. Vinegar as he went on with his cane, "and my legs were very weary. I could not have done better."

As he drew near to the forest where he had left his wife he heard an owl on a tree laughing, "Hoo, hoo, hoo!" Then it called out his name and he stopped to ask what it wanted.

"Mr. Vinegar," said the owl, "you foolish man, you blockhead, you simpleton! you went to the fair and laid out all your money in buying a cow. Not content with that, you changed the cow for some bagpipes on which you could not play and which were not worth one tenth as much as the cow. Ah, foolish, foolish man! Then you no sooner had the bagpipes than you changed them for the gloves that were worth not one quarter as much as the bagpipes ; and when you got the gloves you exchanged them for a cane, and now for your forty guineas you have nothing to show but that poor miserable stick which you might have cut in any hedge. Hoo, hoo, hoo, hoo, hoo!"

The bird laughed loud and long, and **Mr.** Vinegar became very angry and threw his cane at its head. The cane lodged in the tree, and Mr. Vinegar returned to his wife without money, cow, bagpipes, gloves, or stick, and she said things to him that he liked even less than what the bird had said.

THE GIANT OF THE BLACK MOUNTAINS

ONCE upon a time there was a hunter and he had one son. While this son was still a little boy the hunter said to his wife, " My dear, our child will no doubt grow up to be a hunter just as I am, and if I should not be alive when that time comes I wish you would take care to tell him that he must not go to the Black Mountains to hunt; for evil befalls whoever goes thither."

Soon afterward the hunter died, and in time his son grew up and became a hunter as his father had been before him. Then his mother said, " Son, your father commanded me that I should warn you not to go to the Black Mountains to hunt."

But the son saw no good reason why he should not hunt there as well as elsewhere, and one day he took his bow and arrows, mounted his horse and rode to the Black Mountains. At length he was among the lofty, forest-clad ranges, and he could not perceive but that they were perfectly peaceful

and free from danger. "What could my father
have meant by his warning?" he said to himself,

and he kept riding on until suddenly a huge giant
appeared before him.

"How now!" shouted the giant, "have you
never heard of me that you dare to come and hunt

on my ground?" and he picked up three great rocks
and hurled them in quick succession at the intruder;
but the young man contrived to dodge them, and
fitting an arrow to his bow he shot the giant and
killed him.

"I understand my father's warning now," said
the young man; "but as this monster is no longer
to be feared I will seek out his dwelling and see
what treasure it contains."

So he went farther into the mountains and presently came to a magnificent castle. When he drew
near to the entrance a beautiful maiden appeared at
a window and he addressed her and asked to whom
the castle belonged.

"Its owner is a great giant who will soon come
and tear you in pieces," she replied. "How dare
you venture among these terrible mountains?"

"The giant is dead," said the young man. "I
have killed him."

"Ah then!" cried she, "I am free. I have
been his prisoner for many years, and you are
my deliverer. Wait where you are and I will
come down and unlock the castle gates and let
you in."

She soon had the gates open and bade the young
man welcome, and after he had led his horse to the

stables the beautiful maiden conducted the young man into the palace. Then she told him she was the daughter of a prince, and that the giant had stolen her and that she had almost despaired of help ever reaching her. They talked together for a long time, and they liked each other so well that before they got through talking the young man asked the princess to be his wife.

"I am willing," said she, "and we can live here in the giant's castle."

"Yes," said he, "and I can go out hunting every day among the mountains."

But there was an old witch woman who had a hut in a wild glen not far from the castle, and when she knew that the giant was dead she went secretly to the body and administered some magic medicine that brought the giant to life. "Giant," said she, when she had restored him, "the young man who slew you is now in your castle. Go home and punish him as he deserves."

"No," said the giant, "I want nothing more to do with him. He is too clever with his bow and arrows to suit me, and I shall keep as far away from him as I can."

"Well, then," said the witch, "the task of disposing of him falls to me; for I do not intend to have him staying here in the mountains, if there is any way to prevent it."

"The quicker you get rid of him the better," said the giant. "Send him away on some errand from which he can never come back."

"That is just what I will do," responded the witch, "and I promise you in three days' time he will be gone to return no more."

Then the witch went to the palace and asked to be hired as a servant, and work was given her in the kitchen. It did not take her long to discover how fond the young man was of the princess, and on her third day at the palace she managed to put something into the food the princess ate that made her sick. No sooner was this accomplished than the witch said to the young man, "I fear your princess will die."

"Oh, no," cried he, "she must not die. We must make her well again."

"But there is only one thing can cure her," said the witch, "and that is the Melon of Life."

"Then I will get the Melon of Life," said he, "and I will start for it at once."

So he travelled all day long and in the evening he came to the house of an old man, who gave him lodging for the night. He told the old man the errand he was on, and the old man said, "Son, you are deceived. The expedition is a fatal one. Do not go."

But the young man would not be persuaded to turn back. "Well," said the old man, "if you must have your way I will give you three things to take with you. Here is a little jug of water, and here is a comb, and here is a knife. The Melon of Life is guarded by fifty giants, and if they pursue you throw these things behind you one at a time as there is need."

The young man took the jug and the comb and the knife and went his way, and at last he came to the garden of the fifty giants. He succeeded in getting into it without being seen, and there he found the Melon of Life. This he picked, and he wasted not a moment in starting on his return journey, but in getting through the garden hedge he cracked some dry twigs, and that alarmed the giants.

They looked around the garden to learn what had caused the noise, and soon perceived that the Melon of Life was gone. Then they set off in pursuit of the young man. When he saw that they were getting near him he threw the jug behind him. The water in it flowed out and covered the land he had just passed over with a great lake.

While the giants were going around this lake he gained quite a distance on them. But presently he saw them coming again. Then he threw the comb behind him and there sprang up a thick jungle through which the giants had great difficulty in forcing their way.

Thus he gained again on his pursuers. But they at length came out of the jungle and were on his trail once more. As soon as he saw them he threw the knife behind him, and the land in his rear was covered with thorn bushes, and the thorns were like sharp knives.

This time the young man got entirely away from the fifty giants and returned to the Black Mountains. However, during his absence, the giant whom the witch had restored to life had taken possession of the castle, and the princess had recovered from her sickness and was locked up in a dungeon.

When the young man approached the castle the giant chanced to be standing at the gates and saw him while he was still at a distance. The giant was very much startled, for he never expected that the young man would come back, and as he did not care to meet him he ran off at once to the forest.

The young man at sight of the giant knew that things had gone wrong while he was away, and he made all haste into the castle, and the first thing he did was to release the princess. She was now quite well and did not need the Melon of Life and he locked it up in a closet.

They did not suspect the treachery of the witch woman and she continued to work in the kitchen. Every night she went to see the giant in the forest, and they plotted how to get rid of the young man once more. "I can never go back to my castle while he is alive," said the giant, "but I know an easy way to dispose of him."

"What is it?" asked the witch.

"If you can pull three hairs from his head he will die," replied the giant.

"Very well," said the witch, "I will pluck the three hairs, though it may be some time before I find a good opportunity."

So she watched and watched until one day the young man fell asleep on a couch in the great hall of the castle. Then the witch stole softly up to the couch, and selecting three hairs suddenly pulled them out. Immediately the young man's sleep became death, and the witch hurried off to tell the giant of what she had accomplished.

While she was gone the princess came in and found the young man dead, and she cried and was

The witch hurried off to tell the giant of what she had accomplished

very sad. But at last she thought of the Melon of Life locked in the closet and ran and brought it and held it before the young man's nostrils. No sooner did she do that than the young man sneezed seven times and sat up saying, "Oh, what a sound sleep I have had!"

"Sleep!" exclaimed the princess, "it was a sleep out of which you would never have awakened had it not been for the Melon of Life."

Then she told him of how she had found him perfectly lifeless. "There is some villainy in this," said he, "and we had better be on the watch."

So he got his bow and arrows, and he and the princess went up on a tower to look around and see if any danger threatened. They had not been long there when they perceived the giant and the witch coming from the forest. Then the young man let fly an arrow and it hit the witch and that was the end of her. The giant did not wait for him to shoot another arrow. He hastened away as fast as he could go and was never seen in the Black Mountains again, and the young man and the princess lived very happily in the castle ever after.

LAZY JACK

ONCE upon a time there was a boy whose name was Jack, and he lived with his mother in a little house on the borders of a village. They were very poor and the woman kept busy day in and day out at her spinning-wheel; but Jack did no work at all. He would lie in the sunshine when the weather was warm, and when the weather was cold he would sit beside the fire.

Time passed along and Jack grew to be a young man, but still his mother could not get him to do anything for her, and finally, just after breakfast one Monday morning, when she was beginning her spinning and Jack had settled himself comfortably in the chimney-corner, she said to him, "Jack, unless you begin to work I shall turn you out of the house for good and all, and you will have to get your living as best you may."

Lazy Jack did not care to run the risk of losing his home. "The only safe thing for me to do," thought he, "is to find a job at once," and he got up and went to a neighboring woodcutter and hired himself for the day. When evening came the woodcutter gave the lad a penny for his services, and Jack set off for home well satisfied; but he had never had money before and he handled it so carelessly that in crossing a narrow foot-bridge over a brook he dropped the penny into the water. The brook was deep, yet he could see the penny lying on the bottom and he poked about with a stick hoping to get it out. That only stirred up the mud, and soon the penny was hopelessly lost. Then Jack went on home and told his mother what had happened.

"You stupid boy!" said she, "you should have put it in your pocket."

"I'll do so next time," said Jack.

On Tuesday morning Jack went and hired himself to a dairyman. When evening came the dairyman gave him a quart pail full of milk for his services. "Now," said Jack, "I must not lose this milk as I did my penny. Mother told me I should have put what I got in my pocket, and I will this time. My jacket pockets are large and deep, and I think the pail will go in very well."

So he put the pail of milk into one of his jacket pockets and walked off home; and by the time he got there the milk was all spilled.

"Dear me!" said his mother, "you should have carried it on your head."

"I 'll do so next time," said Jack.

On Wednesday morning Jack went and hired himself to a farmer. When evening came the farmer gave him a cream cheese for his services. " Now," said Jack, " I must not lose this cheese as I did the milk yesterday. Mother told me I should have carried what I got on my head, and I will this time."

So he took the cheese and put it on his head; but the day was warm, and the cheese melted, and some of it dropped off along the way and the rest was matted in his hair.

"You foolish fellow," said his mother, "you should have carried it in your hands."

"I 'll do so next time," said Jack.

On Thursday morning Jack went and hired himself to a baker. When evening came the baker gave him a large tom-cat for his services. " Now," said Jack, " I must not lose this tom-cat as I did the cream cheese yesterday. Mother told me I should have carried what I got in my hands, and I will this time."

So he took up the cat and carried it along in his hands; but pussy began to scratch, and the tighter he gripped it the worse it clawed, until he had to let it go. As soon as he reached home Jack told his mother how the cat got away, and she said, "You silly lad, you should have tied it with a string and dragged it along after you."

"I'll do so next time," said Jack.

On Friday morning Jack went and hired himself to a butcher. When evening came the butcher gave him a nice leg of mutton for his services. "Now," said Jack, "I must not lose this mutton as I did the tom-cat yesterday. Mother told me I should have tied a string to what I got and dragged it along after me, and I will this time."

So he tied a string to the leg of mutton and dragged it along after him in the dirt, and when he got home he found the mutton was spoiled. His mother was more out of patience with him than ever. "You ninny-hammer," said she, "you should have carried it on your shoulder."

"I'll do so next time," said Jack.

On Saturday morning Jack went and hired himself to a cattle-keeper. When evening came the cattle-keeper rewarded him for his services with a little donkey that was too old to be of any more use on the farm. "Now," said Jack, "I must not lose this donkey as I did that leg of mutton yesterday. Mother told me I should have carried what I got on my shoulder, and I will this time."

Jack was a stout fellow, and after considerable trouble he succeeded in hoisting the donkey to his shoulders and started for home. As it happened, he had to pass the mansion of a rich man whose only daughter was deaf and dumb. She had never laughed in her life, and the doctors said unless she was made to laugh she could not hope to have either speech or hearing to the end of her days. So everything was done that could be thought of to make her laugh, but nothing was accomplished. At last the father proclaimed that the first man who succeeded in making his daughter laugh should have her for his wife.

When Jack came along with the donkey on his shoulders the young lady was looking out of the window, and the sight was so strange and comical that she began to laugh very heartily, and im-

mediately she could speak and hear. Her father was
overjoyed, and he sent for Jack and told him how
things were, and Jack married the daughter and was
thus made a rich gentleman. He and his wife had
a beautiful home, and Jack's mother lived with them
in great happiness for the rest of her days.

THE ELVES AND THE SHOE-
MAKER

THERE was once a shoemaker who, though he worked very hard and was very honest, yet could not earn enough to live on. At last all his money was gone and he had the leather for only one more pair of shoes. That evening he cut the leather to have it ready to make into shoes the next day. "Alas!" said he, "things are in a bad way; but I've done the best I could, and now I may as well go to bed."

So he went to bed and fell asleep. Early in the morning he sat down to his work, when, to his great astonishment, there stood the shoes all made on the table. The good man knew not what to say or think of this strange event. He looked at the workman-ship. "Not a false stitch in the whole job," said he. "How neat and true. It is better work than I could do myself."

Presently a customer came in, and the shoemaker showed him the new pair of shoes. The customer

examined them and was so much pleased with them
that he willingly paid a higher price than usual.
With this money the shoemaker bought leather
enough to make two pairs more. In the evening he
cut out the work and went early to bed, that he
might be up and start making the shoes at daybreak
on the morrow. But when he rose with the first
light in the morning, there on the table were the two
pairs of shoes all finished. Buyers came in who
paid him handsomely for the shoes, and he had the
money to buy leather for four pairs more. He cut
out the work again in the evening, and found it
finished the next morning. Thus matters went on
for some time — whatever leather was got ready
in the evening was always made into shoes by
daylight, and the good man soon became quite
prosperous.

One evening, shortly before Christmas, as the
shoemaker and his wife were sitting by the fire
chatting together, he said to her, " I would like to
stay up and watch to-night and see who it is that
comes and does my work for me."

" I think that is a very good plan," said his wife,
" and I will stay up with you."

So they left a light burning and hid themselves in
a corner of the room behind a curtain and watched

what should happen. They saw nothing unusual until the clock struck twelve. Then two little elves slipped in at the door and sat down on the shoe-

maker's bench. They took up the work that was cut out, and how their fingers flew! · They rapped and tapped and stitched away at such a rate that the shoemaker was all amazement and could not take his eyes off them for a moment. Not once did they stop till the job was finished and the shoes stood ready for use on the table.   The elves were through long before daybreak.   However, they did not loiter, but at once bustled out of the house.

The next day the wife said to the shoemaker, "Those little men have made us rich and we ought to be thankful to them and do them a good office in return.   I tell you w'nat I will do—I will make them each a suit of clothes, and you can make each of them a little pair of shoes."

"Yes," said the shoemaker, "and we will have the things ready to give them for Christmas."

So the shoemaker made the little shoes, and his wife made the clothes, and the night before Christmas they laid these things on the table, instead of the leather which was usually put there.   Then they hid behind the curtain to watch what the little elves would do.   The clock struck twelve, and in they came and were going to sit down to their work ; but when they saw the clothes lying on the table for them, they picked them up and laughed and danced and were greatly delighted.   For a little while they capered and jumped about as merry as could be, shaking the clothes and looking them over, and singing,

> "Now we've clothes so fine and neat,
>   Why cobble more for others' feet ?"

Then, with the clothes in their hands, they danced out of the door, and they never came to the house again.   But everything went well with the shoemaker from that time as long as he lived.

THE WISE MEN OF GOTHAM

JOHN BLACK and Thomas Brown were two men of Gotham. They were neighbors, but they were not good friends. One day when Thomas was returning home from Nottingham market he met John on Nottingham bridge and called out roughly, "Where are you going, man?"

"That's none of your business," replied John, "but I don't mind telling you that I am going to Nottingham to buy sheep."

"Buy sheep!" said Thomas, "and which way will you bring them home?"

"Oh," responded John, "I will bring them over this bridge."

"No you won't," said Thomas. "I'm going to stay right here and stop them."

"You'd better not try any tricks of that sort!" exclaimed John, "or it will be the worse for you."

"I'm not afraid of your threats!" shouted Thomas, "and I say again, I'll never let you drive your sheep across this bridge."

" You will ! " yelled John.

" I won't ! " declared the other.

Each man carried a stout cane, and as they talked

they swung their canes in the air and thumped with
them on the ground.

" If you act like that," said John, " you will
make my sheep jump over the side of the bridge
into the water and they will drown."

"Let them drown," said Thomas. "I don't care. You can take them home some other way."

"No, I shall not!" said John, "I shall bring them across this bridge."

"You will get a rap on your head with my cane if you do," said Thomas.

While they were quarrelling another man of Gotham came from the market leading a horse with a bag of meal on its back. He stopped on the bridge and listened to learn what the trouble was between his two neighbors. "How is this?" said he — "you are ready to come to blows over some sheep; but I see not a single sheep for you to fight about."

"No," explained the other two, "they are not bought yet."

"Ah, foolish men!" said the newcomer. "Where is your common-sense? Here, lift this bag of meal from the horse to my shoulders and I will show you what I think of you."

They did as he suggested, and then he went to the side of the bridge, untied the mouth of the bag and shook all his meal out into the river. "Now, neighbors," said he, "how much meal is there in my bag?"

"Why, surely," replied they, "there is none at all."

"Quite right!" said he, "and just as much wit is there in your two heads to stir up a strife about a thing you have not."

So the three men went their ways, and which was the wisest of these three persons, do you think?

THE SALT FISH AND THE EEL

THE men of Gotham were very fond of salt fish, and they bought a great many of them. There was, indeed, no meat food they had on their tables oftener. Of course the cost was considerable, and one time, about the beginning of winter, the men of Gotham got together to consider how to save this expense.

"We have a nice large pond right in the middle of our town," said one man; "why not raise our own fish?"

"Yes, it is a good pond," said another, "but where would we get the fish to stock it with?"

"That is easily done," responded the first man. "You well know how fish multiply. Have we not in our homes many fish not yet eaten? Put those in the pond and let them breed, and next year we shall have a plenty. We will not need to go to market for our salt fish, but will catch them as we want them from our pond."

"Good! good!" cried the men of Gotham clapping their hands and stamping their feet. "Let every man who has salt fish left cast them into the pond!"

"I have many white herrings," said one.

"I have many sprats," said another.

"I have many red herrings," said another.

So they all told what salt fish they had and said, "Yes, yes, throw them into the pond and we shall fare like lords next year!"

Without farther delay the salt fish were put into the pond, and when spring came the men of Gotham thought the fish must have multiplied and that it was time to take some of them out. So they dragged the pond with a net and drew it to the shore expecting to find it full of fish, but it was empty. Again and again they dragged it through the pond, yet do what they would they could not catch any fish. However, at last a large fat eel was found in the net.

"Ah!" said they all, "a mischief on this eel, for he has eaten all our fish."

"And now what shall we do with him?" said they.

"Kill him!" said one.

"Chop him into pieces!" said another.

"Not so," said another; "let us drown him!"

"Be it so!" said all, and the men of Gotham

rowed their boat out to the middle of the pond and
threw the eel overboard into the deep water.

When they saw the eel wriggling down toward the
bottom one man said, "Do you notice how frightened he is? See how he squirms and twists with
terror."

" He may squirm and twist as much as he pleases,"
said another man.   " He must shift for himself
now."

"Yes," said they all, " he shall have no help
from us ; " and they left the eel to drown.

A MISSING MAN FOUND

ONCE upon a time twelve men of Gotham went fishing in the stream that supplied the town pond, and sometimes they fished from the shore, and sometimes they waded out into the stream to get better positions from which to cast their lines. As they were coming back one of them said, " We have ventured much this day wading. I pray God that none of us that did come from home be drowned."

" Let us see about that," said a second man. " Twelve of us came out this morning. I will count and see if there be twelve going back."

So he counted, " One, two, three, four, five, six, seven, eight, nine, ten, *eleven*."

But he forgot to count himself. " I can make no more than eleven," said he. " Surely, one of us is drowned."

Then the other men counted, but each forgot to count himself and could find only eleven. " Alas! "

said one to another, " there is no doubt about it. One of us is drowned."

They went back to the stream where they had been fishing and looked up and down for him that was drowned and made great lamentation.   By and by a man of Nottingham came riding past.   " What are you looking for there ? " he asked, " and why are you so sorrowful ? "

" Oh," said they, " this day we came to fish in this stream, and there were twelve of us, and one is drowned, for now there are but eleven of us."

" Count me how many of you there be," said the stranger.

One of the men of Gotham counted, and as he did not count himself he made eleven.

" Well," said the stranger, " what will you give me if I will find the twelfth man ? "

" Sir," said they, " we will give you all the money we have."

" Give me the money," said the Nottingham man.

When the money was safe in his pocket he said, " Now pass in front of me ; and he began with the first man and hit him a crack on the shoulders with his whip.

" There is one," said he.

The next one he cracked with his whip likewise. "There are two," said he; and so he served them all down to the last, whom he gave an extra hard blow and said, "Here is your twelfth man."

"God bless your heart!" said all the company; "you have found our neighbor."

THE KETTLE THAT WOULD NOT WALK

ONE day a Gotham man was getting ready to go to market, and his wife said to him, "Husband, we need a new iron kettle for the fireplace. Don't fail to buy one."

So the man bought a kettle at Nottingham, and toward evening he took it on his arm and started for home. But the kettle was heavy, and at length his arm grew tired with carrying it and he set it down. While he was resting he noticed that the kettle had three legs. "What a pity I did not see those legs before!" cried the man. "Here you have three legs and I have but two, and yet I have been carrying you. 'T were fairer that you had carried me. Well, you shall take me the rest of the way, at least."

Then he seated himself in the kettle and said, "Now, go on; I am all ready;" but the kettle stood stock still on its three legs and would not move.

"Ah!" said the man, "you are stubborn, are you? You want me to keep on carrying you, I suppose; but I shall not. I will tell you the way and you can stay where you are until you get ready to follow me."

So he told the kettle where he lived and how to get there, and then off the man went. When he reached home his wife asked him where the kettle was.

"Oh, it will be along in good time," he replied.

"And what do you mean by that?" said she.

"Why," said he, "the kettle I bought has three legs, and was better able to walk here from Nottingham market than I who have but two legs. Yet I never noticed it had legs until I was nearly here. Then I told it to walk the rest of the way itself, for I would carry it no farther."

"Where did you leave it?" asked the wife.

"You need not be anxious," responded the man.

"I told it the way, and it will be along in good time, as I said before."

"And where did you leave it?" again asked the wife.

"At Gotham bridge," he replied.

She was not so sure about its coming as he was and she hurried off to get it, and when she brought it home the man said, "I am glad you have it safe, wife, for I have been thinking while you were gone that it might have taken a notion to walk back to Nottingham if we had left it alone there in the road much longer."

THE LITTLE HORSE AND ITS KIND MASTER

THERE was once a man of Gotham who started for market with two bushels of wheat, and the wheat was in a bag laid across his horse's back, and the man sat just behind the bag. But he had not gone far when another man of Gotham called to him from a wayside field and said, "Your horse is small, neighbor, for so much of a load. Why do you not walk and lead it?"

"That is what I would do," replied the first man; "but my foot is lame and I cannot walk very well."

"Then if you must ride," said the other, "I think you might take the bag of wheat on your shoulder so the horse would not have to carry that, too."

"Why, so I could," said the first man; and he hoisted the bag of wheat to his shoulder and there he carried it all the way to market.

"Ah," said he, when he reached his destination, "how my little horse does pant and sweat! I did well to share the work with it, for I see clearly that the horse has had burden enough carrying me without having also to carry this heavy bag of wheat."

THE GOTHAM MEN AND THE CUCKOO

THE men of Gotham thought that the cuckoos were the finest songsters of all the birds. "The only thing I do not like about the cuckoos," said one man, " is that they do not sing all the year through. They stay with us only a few months in the spring and summer, and then they fly away."

" Well," said another man, "why not catch one of the birds and keep it with us always? "

This plan was pleasing to the men of Gotham and they said, " Yes, we will catch a cuckoo and we will fix a place for it near the middle of the village, so that we can all hear it sing every day."

They went to work at once and in a corner of a field built a stout paling fence more than six fee high and filled in all the crevices with brush and willow twigs. " No bird can get through that fence," said they when it was finished.

Then they caught a cuckoo and put it inside of the fence, and they said to the cuckoo, "You must sing there all through the year, or you shall have neither meat to eat nor water to drink."

But the cuckoo as soon as it was set free inside of the fence flew away.

"A vengeance on the bird!" exclaimed the men of Gotham. "We did not make our fence high enough."

THE HARE THAT WAS SENT
TO YORK

ONCE upon a time the men of Gotham wanted to send a message to their landlord who lived in York. This was before there were any railroads or mails, and if a message was to be sent, some one must go with it. But none of the citizens of Gotham wished to go as far as York. "How, then, shall we send our message?" said they.

"I caught a hare to-day," said one man, "and hares are very swift of foot, you know. Why not let him carry it?"

"Very good," said all; "we will get the letter ready and we will tell the hare the right way to go and he shall carry it."

So the letter was written and sealed and tied to the hare's neck. "First you go to Nottingham," said they to the hare, "and then you go straight on by the main highway to York, and the letter is marked for our landlord who lives near York Cathedral.

You can ask when you get there which house is his. Commend us to him and give him the letter."

The hare, as soon as he was out of their hands, left the road and ran off across a field, and some of the men of Gotham cried out after it, "Stop! stop! You must go to Nottingham first."

" Let the hare alone," said one of those who was in the company. " He can tell a nearer way than the best of us all. Let him go."

"Yes," said another, " that is a clever creature. Let him alone. He will not keep the highway for fear of dogs."

THE CRANE IN THE WHEAT-FIELDS

ONCE, in the summer, when the wheat had grown high, a crane was often seen in the fields belonging to the Gotham townsmen, walking up and down in the grain patches to catch frogs. This troubled the men of Gotham greatly. "See how big he is," said one, "and look at the legs of him. He is treading down a vast deal of grain, to be sure."

"We must drive the animal away, or we shall have no harvest," said another.

"Very true," said still another, "and the quicker the better. Let us appoint Tom Thacker, the shepherd, for the job. He is used to much walking and the work would suit him well."

So Tom Thacker, the shepherd, was appointed to go into the fields and chase the bird out. But as he went in after the crane his neighbors noticed that his feet were very broad and large, and though he scared off the bird, he at the same time trampled down a great deal of wheat.

"That will never do," said one of the townsmen, and the men of Gotham puzzled their brains for some better method.

At last one of them said, "The thing to do is this — some of us must carry the shepherd when he goes into the grain again, so that he shall not tread it down."

"Yes, yes," cried the others, "that is the proper thing to do, and why did we not think of that before, I wonder?"

Then they took a stout fence gate off its hinges, had the shepherd sit down on it, and eight men lifted the gate on their shoulders and carried it through the fields of wheat, where the crane was in the habit of resorting, that the shepherd might scare the bird away.

"The shepherd will not trample down any more of our grain with his big feet now," said the men of Gotham.

THE MEN OF GOTHAM AND
THE WATCH

ONE day a number of Gotham men were walking along the road when they found a watch lost by some traveller. None of them had ever seen such a queer thing before, and they looked at it with great surprise and curiosity. Suddenly, one of the party who had taken the watch in his hand noticed that a ticking sound came from the inside of it.

"Do you hear that?" said he. "The thing must be possessed by an evil spirit."

He was very much frightened and threw the watch away. Not one of the party dared touch it now. But the oldest among them, more courageous than the rest, picked up a large stone and hammered the watch until it was entirely smashed. Of course that stopped its ticking. The brave man then kneeled down and laid his ear to the watch and listened.

"Ah," said he proudly to his companions when he heard no sound, "I have taught him to keep quiet. That stone did the business."

So they all rejoiced that they had destroyed an evil spirit and went away leaving the watch on the ground.

THE CHEESES THAT RAN
AWAY

THERE was a man of Gotham who filled a
sack with cheeses and started off for Nottingham market to sell them. He carried
the sack on his back, and when he became tired he
sat down by the wayside to rest. Thus he went on
until he reached the summit of the last hill he had
to climb before he came to Nottingham bridge.
There he rested, and when he rose to continue his
journey a cheese slipped out of the sack and rolled
down the hill toward the bridge.

"Ah! Mr. Cheese," said the man, "so you can
run to market alone, can you? I wish I had known
that before. It would have saved me the trouble
of carrying you. Well, then, if you can go to
market alone, so can the other cheeses, and I will
send them along after you."

So he laid down his sack, took out the cheeses,
and one by one rolled them down the hill. As the

last one spun down the road he shouted, " I charge
you all to meet me at the market-place."

Some of the cheeses went into one bush, and some
went into another bush, but the man did not notice
that, and he trudged on cheerfully to the market
expecting the cheeses would meet him there. All
day long he loitered about the market, and as even-

ing approached be began to inquire among his friends and neighbors and other men if they had seen his cheeses come to the market.

" Who should bring them?" asked one of the marketmen.

" Nobody," replied the man of Gotham. " They would bring themselves. They know the way well enough."

" Why, then, are they not here?" said the marketman.

" A plague on them all!" cried the owner of the cheeses. " It has just occurred to me what the trouble is. I did fear, when I saw them start off so fast, that they would run beyond the market, and I am sure they must be now miles away on the road to York."

Forthwith he hired a horse and rode in all haste to York in pursuit of his cheeses. But he did not find them at York, nor has he been able to discover whither they ran even to this day.

THE LOST LEGS

SEVERAL men of Gotham once sat down on the ground in a circle, and when they wanted to get up their legs were so intermingled that no one could make out which were his.

"Alas!" said they, "what a pity that we sat down thus. We shall never again be able to rise and walk — that is quite plain."

So they remained sitting there very sorrowful and quiet until they saw a traveller passing. They called to him and asked if he could tell them how they might find their legs. The traveller took his cane and pointed out to each man his feet. "Now," said he, "you know where your feet are, all you need do is to stand on them."

But his explanations only confused the men of Gotham the more. "It is of no use," said they. "However, we thank you, sir, for your good intentions."

"Oh, well," said the traveller, "I have n't given up yet. I 'll try one more plan."

Then he struck one of the men smartly on the legs with his cane, and that man discovered which legs were his in no time and scrambled away. The traveller served another man in like manner, and a

third, and so on till every man tumbled out of the heap and got on his feet.

"How remarkable!" said one of them, "that with the rap of a stick we should discover our legs so quickly when with all our thinking we could not have determined which were which had we sat there a hundred years."

THE HIDING OF THE CHURCH BELL

THE men of Gotham were once greatly scared by a report that enemies were about to invade their country. They were anxious to save as much as they could from falling into the hands of the invaders; and first of all they decided to save their church bell, which they prized more than anything else. After a great deal of trouble they succeeded in getting it down out of the church steeple; but what to do with it then was far from easy to determine.

"Where shall we hide it so the enemy cannot find it?" asked one of another.

At last some one said, "Let us sink it in the deepest part of our pond."

"Agreed!" said his fellows, and they dragged the bell down to the shore of the pond and got it aboard a boat.

Then they rowed out to the middle of the pond and hoisted the bell overboard. After it had dis-

appeared the worthy citizens of Gotham began to
think they had been hasty. "The bell is now truly
safe from the enemy," said they; "but how are we
to find it when the enemy has left us?"

One of them, who was wiser than the rest, sprang
up and cried, "That is easy enough.   All we have
to do is to cut a mark where we dropped it in!"

He snatched a knife from his pocket and cut a
deep notch in the side of the boat where the bell

had been thrown overboard. "It was right here that we heaved the bell out," said he.

Then the men of Gotham rowed back to the shore, fully assured that they would be able to find their bell by the mark on the side of the boat.

The End

New Books for the Young

WITH SPURS OF GOLD

By FRANCES N. GREENE and DOLLY WILLIAMS KIRK.
With illustrations. 12mo. Decorated cloth, $1.50.

A BOOK of stories of famous knights, including the tales
of the deeds of Roland and Oliver, the Cid, Godfrey de
Bouillon, Richard Cœur de Lion, the Chevalier Bayard, and
Sir Philip Sidney in a series of narratives which, while in a
way historical studies, are full of life, action, and entertain-
ment, as well as instructive information.

MEN OF OLD GREECE

By JENNIE HALL, author of "Four Old Greeks," etc.
With eight full-page plates and numerous illustrations
in the text. 16mo. Decorated cloth, $1.50.

THIS volume gives four important chapters on Greek his-
tory and biography, written with a graphic presentation
that will make the stories permanent possessions of child
readers. The first is the story of Leonidas, followed by the
story of Marathon and Salamis. The third part is devoted
to a biographical narrative of Socrates, and the closing portion
tells of the rebuilding of the Acropolis, giving a pen picture of
Phidias and his working artists.

WILDERNESS BABIES

By JULIA A. SCHWARTZ. With sixteen full-page illustrations by John Huybers and other artists. 12mo.
Decorated cloth, $1.50.

THE adventures and perils of sixteen common mammals are
so vividly told that what would ordinarily be set forth as
dull, prosaic fact is here woven into a tale pulsating with life
and interest. A graceful style, enriched with charm and
fancy, and a real feeling for wild nature and child sympathies,
combine to make this treatment fresh and telling. The author
has a gift rarely vouchsafed to writers for the young.

New Books for the Young

THE OAK-TREE FAIRY BOOK

Edited by CLIFTON JOHNSON. With eleven full-page
plates and seventy-five smaller illustrations from
pictures by Willard Bonte. Crown 8vo. Decorated
cloth, $1.75.

HERE are the old favorites in a version especially suited
for the home fireside. The interest, the charm, and all
the sweetness have been retained; but savagery, distressing
details, and excessive pathos have been dropped. Its clean
text combined with its beautiful illustrations make it the
most delightful collection of fairy tales ever published.

BOYS WHO BECAME FAMOUS MEN

Stories of the Childhood of Poets, Artists, and Musicians.
By HARRIET PEARL SKINNER. Illustrated by Sears
Gallagher. 12mo. Decorated cloth, $1.25.

INCIDENTS in the childhood of eight celebrated men —
poets, artists, and musicians — are here wrought into
stories that are interesting for the story's sake. Essentially
the incidents are true, and thus the book is in a measure biographical; but the stories are told with so much animation
and color as to make them as interesting as fiction.

HEROES OF ICELAND

Adapted from Dasent's translation of "The Story of
Burnt Njal," the great Icelandic Saga. With a new
Preface, Introduction, and Notes by Allen French.
Illustrated by E. W. D. Hamilton. 12mo. Deco-
rated cloth, $1.50.

ICELAND in the tenth century, the age of heroic deeds and
of the Change of Faith, is the scene of this story — a story
that is really a simplified version of the great saga first intro-
duced to English-speaking people in the translation by Sir
George Webbe Dasent. The old heathen life, the coming
of Christianity, the mighty struggles of the heroes who
thought it no shame to kill men but great shame to tell an
untruth, — all this is vividly pictured as the saga sweeps on
to its climax.

New Books for Boys

SHIPWRECKED IN GREENLAND

By ARTHUR R. THOMPSON, author of "Gold-Seeking on
the Dalton Trail." With twelve full-page illustrations from photographs. 12mo. Decorated cloth,
$1.50.

AN adventure story with the scene laid in northern waters.
A party of boys with a sea-captain, and an older young
man, find a drifting steamer not far from St. John, and set
out to rescue the stranded passengers and crew. Their adventures on the Greenland and Labrador Coast are vividly
portrayed, and their visit to the Eskimos' villages is instruc-
tively entertaining.

THE BOY CAPTIVE IN CANADA

By MARY P. WELLS SMITH, author of "The Boy Captive
of Old Deerfield," "The Young Puritans Series,"
"The Jolly Good Times Series," etc. Illustrated.
12mo. Decorated cloth, $1.25.

THIS is the second story in the Old Deerfield Series, a
sequel to "The Boy Captive of Old Deerfield," and contains
the stirring adventures and experiences of little Stephen
Williams, the son of the Deerfield minister, during his wan-
derings as a captive with the Indians in Northern Vermont,
and during a Canadian winter spent with his captors. It also
tells of his happy redemption and return.

THE REFORM OF SHAUN

By ALLEN FRENCH, author of "The Junior Cup," "The
Story of Rolf, and the Viking's Bow," etc. Illustrated by Philip R. Goodwin and Charles E. Heil.
12mo. Decorated cloth, $1.00.

TWO appealing dog stories by an author who has written
several successful books for the young— "The Reform of
Shaun" and "Mystic and his Master." Shaun is a young dog
who made himself so troublous in the home in which he was
placed that his master sent him back to the kennels. Then
an older dog gives him good advice, and after that he lives a
sedate dog life. Both stories will appeal strongly to all lovers
of dogs.

New Illustrated Editions of Miss Alcott's Famous Stories

THE LITTLE WOMEN SERIES

By Louisa M. Alcott. Illustrated Edition. With eighty-four full-page plates from drawings especially made for this edition by Reginald B. Birch, Alice Barber Stephens, Jessie Willcox Smith, and Harriet Roosevelt Richards. 8 vols. Crown 8vo. Decorated cloth, gilt, in box, $16.00.

Separately as follows:

1. LITTLE MEN : Life at Plumfield with Jo's Boys
With 15 full-page illustrations by Reginald B. Birch. $2.00.

2. LITTLE WOMEN : or Meg, Jo, Beth, and Amy
With 15 full-page illustrations by Alice Barber Stephens. $2.00.

3. AN OLD-FASHIONED GIRL
With 12 full-page pictures by Jessie Willcox Smith. $2.00.

4. JO'S BOYS, and How They Turned Out
A Sequel to "Little Men." With 10 full-page plates by Ellen Wetherald Ahrens. $2.00.

5. EIGHT COUSINS ; or, the Aunt-Hill
With 8 full-page pictures by Harriet Roosevelt Richards.

6. ROSE IN BLOOM
A Sequel to "Eight Cousins." With 8 full-page pictures by Harriet Roosevelt Richards. $2.00.

7. UNDER THE LILACS
With 8 original full-page pictures by Alice Barber Stephens. $2.00.

8. JACK AND JILL
With 8 full-page pictures from drawings by Harriet Roosevelt Richards. $2.00.

The artists selected to illustrate have caught the spirit of the originals and contributed a series of strikingly beautiful and faithful pictures of the author's characters and scenes. — *Boston Herald.*

Alice Barber Stephens, who is very near the head of American illustrators, has shown wonderful ability in delineating the characters and costumes for "Little Women." They are almost startlingly realistic. — *Worcester Spy.*

Miss Alcott's books have never before had such an attractive typographical dress as the present. They are printed in large type on heavy paper, artistically bound, and illustrated with many full-page drawings. — *Philadelphia Press.*

LITTLE, BROWN, & COMPANY

Publishers, 254 WASHINGTON STREET, BOSTON, MASS.

CPSIA information can be obtained
at www.ICGtesting.com
Printed in the USA
LVHW08s0543150818
587039LV00026B/109/P